from folly

from folly

A TRUE STORY

MATTHEW LOCK PRIDGEN

FOUR
WINDS
BOOKS

Charleston, South Carolina

FROM FOLLY

PUBLISHED BY FOUR WINDS BOOKS
PO Box 21597
Charleston, SC 29413
www.fourwindsbooks.org

The names and identifying details of some
characters in this book have been changed.

For information about discounts for bulk purchases,
please contact Four Winds Books Special Sales:
(843) 323-6822 or sales@fourwindsbooks.org

All Scripture quotations, unless otherwise noted, have been taken from The Holy Bible,
English Standard Version® (ESV®), copyright © 2001 by Crossway, a publishing
ministry of Good News Publishers. Used by permission. All rights reserved.

ISBN 978-0-615-47114-3

Printed in the United States of America
First Edition 2011

To my father,
the poet

PREFACE

This most of all: ask yourself in the most silent hour of your night: must I write? Dig into yourself for a deep answer. And if this answer rings out in assent, if you meet this solemn question with a strong, simple "I must," then build your life in accordance with this necessity.

Rainer Maria Rilke

In 2008, over 275,000 books were published in the United States alone. If that's not scary enough, the total number of unique books in the world has been estimated at 130 million. So when I first sat down to write this book, I couldn't help but feel overwhelmed by the thought that my story would be just one more drop in a bucket that is simply too large to fathom.

Yet I wrote it nonetheless. Because I had to write. Because I have a story to tell. As Maya Angelou once put it, "There is no greater agony than bearing an untold story inside you." This has been my experience over the last six years as I have told my tale hundreds, if not thousands, of times. Everywhere I go, the story has a way of bubbling up from deep inside, and I find myself sharing it whether I intend to or not.

To be honest, I don't always enjoy telling it. There is a place of complete personal tedium from sheer repetition where the words feel so rote that they emerge from my mouth like an automated response. I look to my audience expecting them to be as jaded as I am, only to remember that this is likely the first time they have heard my yarn.

The story is truly stranger than fiction. And while parts of it are quite entertaining, I don't tell it for that reason. I have seen something that has the power to change one's life forever—and I am living proof. More than six years after my failed suicide attempt in the ocean on LSD, I remain sober from alcohol and drugs. I have emerged from the depths of complete insanity and regained a life of meaning and purpose.

This book is an invitation to enter my story, to see what I saw and to thereby gain a new perspective on life itself. My desire is to play the tape through on the choices that nearly destroyed my life, in order to tangibly illustrate where the road I once traveled ends. May it serve then as a warning, a cautionary tale from someone who has peered across the thin veneer of death—and lived to tell about it.

CHAPTER ONE

THE OCEAN

IMAGINE YOU JUST WOKE from a dream. Memories from a world far beyond this one bounce off the walls of your mind, eluding your grasp like minnows in a stream. As your eyes begin to adjust to the early morning light slipping horizontally through the blinds, you fight with all of your being to hold on to an intense but fleeting impression that you have been somewhere wonderful or done something extremely important.

Yet the harder you try to remember, the more this dream world closes to you, leaving you with a head full of images that make no sense whatsoever. You slowly become more aware of the reality that is your bed, your room and your life, and you begin to prepare yourself for just another normal day.

Now imagine that instead of waking up in your bed, this particular morning you awake to find yourself in the middle of the ocean. You are alone and naked, and you see nothing but blue all around. The water is cold, but you have been swimming for hours, so you don't notice. The sky is clear, and the sun hangs motionless directly above you.

There is a single ship off in the distance, yet without any point of reference, it could be miles away. You pipe out of the water, searching with your eyes for land, and finally spot what appears to be the beach where you began your swim. Startled, stranded and confused, you bob up and down in the chopping waves, wondering if you will ever make it back. This is where my story begins.

∞ WIDE AWAKE ∞

IT WAS MAY of 2005. I had just finished my junior year of college and was living at home with my parents in Charleston, South Carolina for the summer. I had been taking large doses of LSD for close to three weeks. While I was no stranger to drugs, this was my first experience with such an intense hallucinogen. Jumping in head first, I took 27 hits of acid over the course of 18 days.

During that time, I came to the conclusion that I was the Messiah, the Second Coming of Jesus Christ. I wasn't religious—just insane. According to my delusion, my primary duty as the Messiah was to drown myself in the ocean so that upon my death, the final day of judgment could come. On that day, every man and woman who has ever lived would stand before God to give account for their lives. The earth as we know it would be destroyed, and the eternal kingdom of God would be established for all time.

Although it seems completely fantastical, somehow this made enough sense in my mind that on the morning of May 29, 2005, I swam out into the Atlantic Ocean to die. My plan was to swim as far away from shore as I could, exhausting all of my strength in the process so that even if I changed my mind at the last second, it would be too late—my fate would already be sealed.

I swam for hours and hours, until I reached the point where I could no longer see land, and then attempted to hold my body under the surface of the sea. Yet ending my life proved to be much harder than I had expected. After a series of failed attempts, I decided that I simply could not kill myself in this way. My mind started spinning, and doubt began to cast its ugly shadow over the veracity of my story. In an attempt to stay calm, I told myself that I would simply swim back to land and reorganize my thoughts there. That's when reality struck.

I don't know if something changed chemically in my brain or if I entered some form of natural shock, but all of a sudden, I was sober as a judge. It was the first truly lucid moment I can remember having since I started on acid weeks before. In fact, I felt more coherent at that moment than I had in a long time, as if two years of drug haze had been lifted in an instant.

I honestly can't explain how someone who had been alone and naked in the middle of the ocean for half a day could suddenly come to the shocking realization that they were, well, alone and naked in the middle of the ocean—yet this was my great epiphany. I awoke from my drug insanity, and in a single moment, all of my acid-tripping, pot-smoking, coke-snorting, ecstasy-rolling, mushroom-eating, pain-pill-popping memories began to melt away like nothing more than an elusive dream.

As I watched my fantasy world dissolve before my very eyes, the desperateness of my situation finally set in. I wasn't Jesus. I was just some naked dude out for a swim. I was alone and tired, and worst of all, I had absolutely no reason to be there, no eternal significance to justify my actions. My self-sabotage suicide plan had been fully set into motion, and I had no means of escape. I was going to die in the ocean.

While my life didn't flash before my eyes, I did immediately think of my parents and all of my family and friends who would be devastated when they heard of my selfish decision to end my life. I imagined the questions they would be doomed to wrestle with for the rest of their lives, forever asking themselves what they had done wrong or how they could have prevented this tragedy from happening.

Yet as overwhelmed as I was by this thought, I realized something else at the very same moment that carried with it even deeper implications. I suddenly knew that eternity was real. The mystery of the eternal had petrified me for practically my whole life and had up to this point caused me to deny its existence. But in that instant—perhaps due to my close proximity to death—I peered across the chasm that separates this life from the next and saw that death is not the end.

A few moments before, when I was still the Messiah, this information had been all well and good. My eternal forecast looked pretty sunny, and I simply could not wait to get to heaven. But now that I was back to reality, back to being a drug-addicted college student committing suicide in the ocean, I knew that my prospects were not bright. *How could someone like me possibly belong in a place like heaven?* No, with eternity looming just around the corner, I was headed straight for hell.

Sheer dread pulsed through my veins. My skin began to crawl as my insides convulsed in horror. Panic robbed me of breath. My greatest fear in the world was about to become a reality, and there was nothing I could do about it. A few moments ago, I wanted to die and couldn't. Now I wanted more than anything to live—but knew that it was too late.

∞ A DELICATE BALANCE ∞

AS FAR BACK AS I can remember, the thought of eternity has been my greatest fear. One of my earliest memories is sitting on the floor of my parents' bedroom gripped with fright, repeating a single phrase over and over to myself: "It's never going to end, it's never going to end, it...is...never...going...to...end." Wave after wave of panic crashed over me, and I knew that I had no means of escape.

These episodes happened quite regularly throughout my childhood and were often strong enough to make me physically ill. First, my breathing would grow shallow, and then my stomach would begin to churn. The pressure would build inside of my chest until I ached to vomit, although I only remember doing so once, in a sink at church.

I never knew when or where this fear would come on, but Sunday mornings were always suspect. As an acolyte, I mapped out an escape route from my seat behind the altar for fear that I wouldn't make it through the service. I imagined myself darting in front of the priests to the side door at the end of the altar rail and escaping into the empty halls of the church, which served as my refuge. I would then head straight for the nearest restroom, find a stall and lock myself in.

Although I never found a true remedy, I did develop a process to cope with the fear and to thereby avoid complete meltdown. First, I would conjure up all of my thoughts on eternity—from pearly gates to fire and brimstone to a vast expanse of nothing—and gather them together into one place. Then, I would visualize myself packing the whole mess into one big scary box, as if I could somehow put all of my terror and dread into permanent storage. Finally, I would picture a wall in my mind and simply put the box on the other side.

While I managed to derive a certain amount of peace from this process, I knew that the fear wasn't wholly gone. The reason why the thought of eternity plagued me so horribly in the first place was due to my realization that it would *never* be gone. Not on this side of death at least. But for the moment, it was out of sight—and out of sight is out of mind. Thus, I learned early on how to push the scary things far away, in the box behind the wall, and then go on with my life the very best I could.

To this day, I still wonder what caused me to be so plagued by the intangible thought of eternity at such a young age. I found monsters and the like to be scary as well, but there was one very important detail about monsters which prevented them from keeping me up at night—they aren't real. All I had to do was remind myself of this fact, and the fear would quickly vanish.

Cockroaches were my second greatest fear, and unlike monsters, they are very real. Particularly in South Carolina. Every night before I went to bed, I made sure that my feet were completely tucked into my covers so that these heartless little critters would be forced to find some other poor kid to torture.

Just as with monsters, though, I possessed an important truth that I used to overcome my panic and slow my breathing when cockroaches would cross my path, namely that they are a whole lot smaller than me. Whenever I saw one, I would stand at a safe distance, take a few deep breaths and ask myself one simple question: *Who should be scared of whom?*

If you are a native South Carolinian, you may be wondering at this point whether I truly am from the Lowcountry or not. After all, the cockroaches here aren't always quite so small. In fact, they could be described as downright gargantuan. I can safely say that I have enough cockroach stories to last me the rest of my life—like the time one shot out of the toilet paper roll and began running in frantic circles at my feet on the bathroom floor. Then there are the flying ones.

But unlike cockroaches or monsters, eternity is neither small nor imaginary. And as a child, I could not seem to get the idea out of my head. My mathematical mind would dote on limits and asymptotes and the little arrows at the end of a time line that signify it going on and on and on into forever.

And while these concepts are abstract and impossible to fully comprehend, I did know one thing for sure—eternity must be real. Otherwise, how could time just end? If you were to arrive at the very last moment in history, what would you call the moment after that? And the one after that? And the one after that? It did not make sense for time to exist one day and then cease to be the next.

There had to be more, and I knew it.

∞   EVIDENCES OF THE ETERNAL   ∞

ALTHOUGH MANY ASPECTS OF this world are temporal, including our finite life spans, there is evidence all around us that points to a deeper and much more lasting reality. In my youth, I discovered several of these "evidences of the eternal" and divided them into three categories: macro-infinity, micro-infinity and time-infinity. While my understanding was basic and strictly Newtonian, these concepts provided my very first glimpse into how the supernatural realm has been embedded in the created order.

The first is macro-infinity, the idea that outer space must go on forever. I realized that if space were finite, then there would have to be a stopping point, a boundary somewhere out there where all things simply cease to be.

I tested the theory by visualizing myself flying through the far reaches of outer space, farther and farther, deeper and deeper. I would fly on and on in my mind until at some point, I would imagine a massive barrier, like a giant steel door, blocking my path. When I reached this door, I would attempt to stop moving and remain on the inside.

Yet each time, my mind would just keep traveling right on through this blockade. I imagined the steel stretching thicker and thicker, but I only went faster and faster until I found myself on the other side, cruising through space as before. After several attempts, I finally conceded that space could not logically have an end and simply stopped trying to imagine it.

The second evidence of the eternal, micro-infinity, represents the complimentary idea that the entire physical world is composed of infinitely complex matter—cells made of atoms, atoms made of quarks, quarks made of sub-quarks and so on.

I envisioned this one in much the same way as I did with macro-infinity, only in reverse. Rather than zooming out into the expanding universe, I imagined myself zooming in on the world through the lens of an extremely powerful microscope.

In my mind's eye, I would increase the magnification over and over again, watching as blades of grass reduced down to single cells and then opened up into a world of swirling sub-atomic particles, which would then be broken into tiny pieces that only got smaller and smaller and smaller.

Each time I focused on any one particular particle, I could always find a way to break it down and zoom in further. Plus, it only made sense to me that physical matter, since it does exist in an infinitely expanding system, would itself be infinitely complex in nature.

The last of the three evidences is time-infinity, which I mentioned briefly before. This idea asserts that time itself could not possibly have a beginning or an end, a concept most simply and graphically represented by the arrows at either end of a timeline.

To test this theory, I would picture myself traveling back in time through the history of the world, all the way to the very first moment of the universe's existence. But as with both of my previous mental pictures, I simply could not stop my mind there and found myself continuing to travel backwards in time, wondering fruitlessly what space looked like before the universe existed.

Next, I would fast forward to the final destruction of our planet, envisioning the sun swelling up into a red dwarf and swallowing the earth whole before finally burning out. Once again, I was not able to stop the scene in my mind from progressing, leaving me with a picture of our desolate solar system and time marching steadily on as before. How could it ever just end?

As a young child, I concluded that these evidences of the eternal could only mean one thing—there must be more to life. How else could one explain the existence of a world that is composed of infinitely complex matter, floating around in an infinitely expanding universe and perpetually moving through an eternal medium?

No, it appeared to me beyond the shadow of a doubt that life was never designed to be finite. Yet while I could not deny my belief in it, the thought of eternal life was precisely the root of my fear. I had plenty of cartoon images from popular culture floating around in my head about what heaven and hell were going to look like, and to be honest, I hated the idea of them all.

Although the depictions of heaven seemed to vary quite a bit, hell was always filled with the standard flames of fire and devils with pitch forks—which to me never appealed. Then to make matters worse, there was one particular line from a Dave Matthews Band song that would play on repeat in my head about how "hell is the closet I'm stuck inside." I really did not want to spend eternity there.

Now being afraid of hell is one thing. That's pretty normal. I unfortunately had the very same feelings about heaven. My fear was based on two impressions which prevailed in my mind of what heaven would be like. The first came from the *Family Circus* comic strip, where heaven was always represented by an image of grandpa playing baseball somewhere up in the clouds.

The second came from a movie that I didn't even like very much called *Bill and Ted's Bogus Journey*, which had a scene depicting heaven as a place where ancient-looking people stood around in white robes all day, playing charades and listening to harp music. The fact that baseball was my least favorite sport did not help. And I just could not figure out how white robes and harp music could possibly improve the quality of any activity, particularly one that involves chasing after fly balls and sliding into home plate. I might be able to stand two or three days of toga baseball, but eternity? How boring could you possibly get? I was ready to rethink the broom closet.

Yet as twisted as my images of life after death may have been, I simply could not deny that I believed in it. All of the evidence pointed to an eternal reality. And while for the most part, I was able to keep my thoughts contained at a safe distance, when they did break loose, I quickly became a mess.

Just like that awful night on the floor of my parents' bedroom, the thoughts would run wild in my mind. *It's never going to end. It's never going to end.* Needless to say, life was a delicate balance for me.

∞ PARALLEL UNIVERSE ∞

THE SUMMER BEFORE sixth grade, my family and I moved down the South Carolina coast from Myrtle Beach to Charleston. Not only was I forced to leave behind my best friends whom I had known my entire life, I also had to make the difficult transition from a public elementary school, where you were lucky to know one or two kids in your class at the beginning of the year, into an elite private school where literally everyone knew everyone. Except me.

I realized immediately upon my arrival that I wasn't in Kansas anymore. For starters, I learned that my tried and true school uniform of Umbro soccer shorts and an oversized t-shirt was not going to fly at this new school, so my mom took me to a department store where I acquired four collared shirts, two pairs of khaki shorts and a belt. I had a particular distaste for collared shirts due to the fact that they reminded me of church, but it appeared as if I had no other option.

It's important to note my incredible lack of fashion sense at this stage in my life, poor even for a sixth grader, which meant that the shirts I chose were not your typical Polos. Since I thought plain old solid colors were boring with a capital B, I chose shirts with a little more pizzazz. Think late '80s, with colors that scream and enough zigging and zagging to go around. That was more my style.

While this new wardrobe made me nervous enough, our family's living situation didn't help to take away the edge. Since we had yet to find a house in Charleston, we decided to move in with my grandparents for a few months. Not that I didn't love them. It's just that I suddenly found myself with two sets of authority figures telling me to eat my vegetables and to put socks on before I caught a cold.

And to make matters worse, they put ice in my milk. Ice. In my milk. So by the time I went to drink it, this once delicious beverage had become diluted and gross. Plus, through the filter of my sixth grade mind, old people were just sort of scary. I always felt like I needed to be on my best behavior when they were around—and they always seemed to be around.

When the first day of school arrived, I was more than ready to get out of the house and even felt a tinge of excitement. Not to say that I didn't have a healthy dose of anxiety mixed in as well, but overall my feeling was one of genuine anticipation. *Maybe this school will be better than my old one,* I thought. *Maybe I'll make a whole bunch of friends right away.*

Of course, it didn't help that I showed up wearing a shirt that would have been a better fit in a modern art museum than at a private elementary school. Let's just say had the tables been turned, I certainly wouldn't have been the first one to go out on a limb and risk my reputation for the sake of the ill-clad new guy. The school year is just too long to make a gamble like that on day one.

Fortunately for me, though, I didn't have to worry for long. I found out that the school administration assigned a host friend to every new student to show them around and help them make the transition into their new environment. My host and I seemed to really hit it off, and straight away, he introduced me to all of his friends. A few days later, he even invited me to spend the night at his house.

But the tide quickly turned when, on the following Monday, he began to mock me in front of one of our classmates. It turns out that it was his mom's idea to ask me over and that he had had no real say in the matter. His warm and gracious front disappeared completely, leaving me to ponder the reasoning behind such a sudden turn. I decided that it must be my new shirts.

By the second week of school, it became evident that this division ran deeper than my avant-garde wardrobe. Not only did I begin to receive the cold shoulder from my student host, his friends made it clear that I was not welcome to sit with them at lunch any longer. Since they had been my only point of contact thus far, I found myself eating alone in the cafeteria for the first time in my life.

For days, I wasn't even able to make it home from school before the tears would start welling up in my eyes. I longed to be back in Myrtle Beach with my lifelong friends who knew and accepted me. It felt as if I had been thrown head first into a parallel social universe where friendships were not simply guided by who sat next to you in class, but by an unspoken system of elitism and exclusivity.

I promptly learned the meaning of the word "clique"—and more importantly that I didn't belong to one. A few days later, one of the kids in my class took it upon himself to reach out to me and began sitting with me at lunch. Our time together was like a solemn refuge in the midst of a violent storm, and he soon became the closest thing to a best friend I ever had in Charleston.

He introduced me to his circle of friends at school, and although the group welcomed me straight away, the damage had already been done. Like a looming black cloud, that deep sense of rejection hovered over me for the rest of my school career.

∞   DOOGIE HOWSER   ∞

As IF FITTING IN among my sixth grade peers wasn't challenge enough, I simultaneously found myself in the throes of a second similar trial. Due to an advanced placement track that I had been taking since primary school, I got put into a seventh grade math class. So for one period each day, I would make my trek across campus to the middle school and try to fit in with yet another population of entirely new faces.

I was in the third grade when I first began joining the class ahead of me for math, so in my mind, this was no big deal. All of the kids at my previous school knew the drill and just accepted it for what it was. In fact, I had always been proud of my math ability and carried a positive attitude with me into my first day of Pre-Algebra.

It didn't take long, though, before all traces of optimism disappeared. I had faced ridicule before, but what I experienced amongst the seventh graders truly surprised me. Incessant taunting seemed to meet me on all sides, and eventually the disdain became so tangible that every moment I spent in the classroom was permeated by a deep sense of unwelcome.

Interestingly enough, it was the smarter students in the class who gave me the most trouble. When my teachers would catch wind of the hazing, they were quick to reassure me that it probably only stemmed from jealousy and that I should, in fact, be flattered. Unfortunately, I didn't ever find much comfort in their words, mostly because I couldn't imagine anyone being jealous of another person's math ability. I mean, there is a reason why you don't see mathematicians on the front of the Wheaties box.

What made the situation even more ominous in my eyes was that although the seventh grade appeared to be just as fractured socially as my class, they managed to unite around one thing—making fun of me. After only a week of school, I gained a disparaging nickname that the entire class used to address me by for the next six years, until they finally graduated at the end of my junior year.

The nickname came from a TV show that aired in the early '90s called "Doogie Howser, MD" about a child prodigy who became a medical doctor at age 14. While I could not see how being advanced one year in one subject elevated me to the level of boy genius, the name stuck. In fact, I'm not so sure that everyone in the class above me actually learned my real name, since many of them still call me by nothing other than "Doogie" to this day.

Now I would be exaggerating if I said that there weren't at least a few exceptions to the rule. I did get "Doogs" quite a bit. And there were a handful of kids who insisted on using my full and proper name, "Doogie Howser." But as for variety, that was about it. The only time I ever heard my real name called in math class was when the teacher addressed me. And that wasn't always a safe bet either.

I've been called many names in my life. Being six foot six, most of them refer to my stature—Sasquatch, Shrek, Big Friendly Giant—but many others are completely random. Like Sunshine. Either way, the point is that I learned early on how to take that sort of thing in stride. Yet for some reason, my new moniker didn't roll off my back quite so easily.

For starters, the name didn't arise from an inside joke between friends like all of the others had up to this point. I didn't know these kids from Adam and felt that I had no recourse with which to defend myself. Since the last thing I wanted to do was make a fuss and come across as a crybaby, I just tried to play it cool and laugh the jokes off as best I could. Plus, the title had been superimposed on me so abruptly that by the time I knew what had hit me, it was too late to object.

The hardest part about being Doogie was the way in which it defined me in the eyes of my peers. Being new on campus, the name became a major part of my identity, following me onto sports teams, clubs and everything else I did at school. It ultimately became like a scarlet letter, proclaiming to all my great transgression of being a math nerd.

So while I continued to fight for a place of belonging among my sixth grade classmates, it felt like the tide was working against me. Since my survival depended on it, I quickly learned the delicate art of deflecting ridicule, detaching myself from any emotional response and wearing a stone face. But every time I heard that nickname, it reminded me of the fact that these people didn't care about me and that this place would probably never feel like home.

One day when I arrived for class, I found a note on my desk with an ultimatum to either leave seventh grade math for good or else pay with my life. I immediately understood that it was supposed to be a joke and didn't spend the rest of the class period looking over my shoulder or anything like that. Yet at the same time, these gestures led me into a depth of rejection that I had never before experienced.

From my perspective, I simply could not understand why we had traveled so far just for me to get picked on. *Myrtle Beach public schools may not have been top of the line*, I thought, *but at least the kids there were nice.* And while our family continued to make trips back on weekends and in the summertime, I inevitably had to let go of that place I once called home.

As the years progressed, I did make some very good friends at my new school, both in my grade and in the grades above. But even so, I was never able to find satisfaction with my status in the social spectrum and desperately wanted to be more popular and well-liked. I developed a root of bitterness in my heart toward those who had rejected me without ever even giving me a chance and harbored that resentment all the way through high school and even into college.

It appeared to me that the social lines had already been drawn and that I had not made the cut. I felt forever doomed to wander aimlessly amongst the nerds and social misfits. And to be honest, I fit in much better there. Video games and chess were two of my favorite activities, and when I made the eighth grade quiz bowl team, I was genuinely excited.

The only problem was that I didn't want to be associated with them, and for one very specific reason. Cool girls hung out with cool guys, not quiz bowl champions. In my mind, this was where the rubber hit the road. All the taunting and teasing in the world didn't mean a thing if you got the girl in the end. At least that's how I saw it.

But by the time high school rolled around, I seemingly hadn't made any social advancement whatsoever. Thus, I resigned myself to the fact that I would probably never fit in with the popular crowd and settled on a new approach instead. Rather than allowing myself to be lumped in with one of the less desirable cliques, I decided to branch out on my own. My reasoning was that if I didn't belong to any one social group, then I would be free to hang out, or hook up, with anyone.

So while I may not have been cool, I did everything necessary to prevent myself from being uncool—by association at least. I slowly began to distance myself from my classmates and sought out girls from other schools who didn't know anything about me or my reputation, and best of all, who had never even heard of the nickname "Doogie."

With them, I had a fresh start. With them, I could be whoever I wanted to be.

∞ THE PHILOSOPHY OF DEATH ∞

OVER THE COURSE OF my high school career, although I didn't notice it happening at the time, my fear of the eternal slowly died down. My growing interest in school and social life created new outlets for my mind to dwell on, and when eternity did come up, I would simply disengage and fix my mind on something else. If a story I was reading contained a chapter on heaven or hell, I would skip it. If I was watching a movie that had a scene depicting the afterlife, I would simply turn it off or leave the room. I wanted nothing to do with eternity.

As I distanced myself from dwelling upon things eternal, I found it necessary to keep all thoughts about God at arm's length as well. I grew more and more skeptical of the church, and even though I went with my family every Sunday, my ears were closed to the words that were spoken.

Instead of keeping an open mind toward the spiritual realm, I wrote it off entirely. I began to gravitate more and more toward the ideas I heard in the science classroom, namely the theory of evolution, and wholeheartedly embraced the thought that human beings are a product of time and chance rather than supernatural design.

I loved the thought of randomness because if life is random, then God is unnecessary. I started to formulate a personal philosophy that completely removed God and eternity from the picture. I figured that since God did not make us, then reality could only be defined in terms of the material world. I rejected the possibility of anything existing beyond the physical matter that I could see, hear, smell, taste or feel.

Over time, I developed this idea and carried it to its logical conclusion, deducing that if reality is defined by physical matter alone, then human consciousness must be nothing more than the product of nerve connections in the brain. Or as Descartes famously articulated, "I think, therefore I am." Thus, when I die and those connections cease to exist, so will my consciousness and hence my entire being.

At that point, my body will begin to rot beneath the surface of the earth until that day long after the end of human civilization when the sun burns out and wipes out all traces of our existence. So regardless of what happens here on earth, time will ultimately blot out everything to the tiniest detail without ever so much as pausing or looking back to give the human race a second thought.

In fact, it is a mathematical principle that any finite number divided by infinity equals zero, represented visually as: $x / \infty = 0$. Since I believed our life spans to be finite, I deduced that my life and yours, along with the lives of everyone else on this planet, will be squashed into nothingness by the eternal expanse of time. That is to say, it will be like we never even existed in the first place.

Therefore, I concluded that no matter how I spend my time on this earth, regardless of whether I set out each day to do good or to do evil, in the end, it will have no effect whatsoever on my eternal destiny. So despite my childhood conviction that human beings are of eternal construct, over the course of time, I effectively convinced myself of the opposite.

I embraced this new worldview not for the sake of rebellion, but honestly because I found it to be the only thing that brought me peace. I particularly liked the idea of dying and leaving nothing behind, that there would be no lasting implications of our actions. That way, for better or worse, everyone on the entire planet would share one common fate, no matter what comes next.

As a result, death itself became a mental refuge for me, and I found myself in a place of serenity for the first time in my life. I even came up with a name for my new belief system, "the philosophy of death," which hinged on two key principles. Without God, there is no eternal life. And without eternal life, there is nothing.

As I considered the implications of this new line of reasoning, I began to see the world through a totally different lens. *If I have no ability to change my ultimate destiny even the slightest bit,* I thought, *then why would I spend my life working hard and making sacrifices for the greater good? If my lifespan truly is finite and will eventually reduce to nothing regardless of how long I live, what's the point in trying at all?*

I saw that regardless of how much money I made in my lifetime or how attractive I was or how many friends I had, regardless of whether I went to church or did community service or gave away everything that I owned, in the end, all of it would be for naught. To me, life felt like sweeping the floor of a building that was about to be demolished.

So instead, I chose to follow the path of least resistance. I lost all motivation to make a difference in the world and soon found myself acting out in ways I never would have imagined before. I even remember breaking into cars late one night just to demonstrate my conviction that God was not hovering over my shoulder, or watching me at all for that matter.

My hope lay not in finding something materially valuable, although I did end up taking a few dollars and a cell phone charger. Rather, my search was for something much more intangible, a way to achieve the freedom to do whatever I wanted, whenever I wanted, without any lasting consequences. And while the crime itself was relatively petty, I came away from the experience more confident of my convictions than ever before.

∞   UNDER THE RADAR   ∞

FROM THIS TIME FORWARD, I rejected the concept of a moral standard and realized that if God is not real, then the idea of judging one set of behaviors and declaring them to be better or worse than another would be impossible. An independent third party, someone completely outside of the human race, would be needed to impose a universal value system, and I simply did not believe that such a being existed.

In my mind, since one behavior was just as valid as the next, I had absolutely no problem lying, cheating, stealing, manipulating or even theoretically murdering to get what I wanted. Since all would be for naught in the end, human life did not possess a whole lot of intrinsic value to me.

Yet despite breaking free from all sense of internal moral obligation, I continued to curb my behavior nonetheless, a phenomenon that can be solely attributed to the set of external restrictions imposed upon my life. These rules were created and enforced by three major sources of authority: my parents, my school and the law of the land.

Although I did not necessarily agree with the boundaries that were established for me, I found it in my best interest to abide by them nonetheless. My cooperation hinged solely on my knowledge of the repercussions that I would face otherwise. Each of these three parties held power over me, including the ability to seriously restrict my freedom, so I obeyed even if only for selfish reasons.

Over time, I became aware of the fact that these authority figures were only able to judge me based on my external actions and not my internal motives. For in a system without God, I am the only person on the planet who can truly know why I do what I do. So even though I continued to play by the rules when others were looking, I was an entirely different person behind closed doors.

The bottom line was that the trust of my parents and teachers represented an extremely valuable asset, so I did my best to hide behind the "good kid" persona. I continued to excel in school and for the most part, minded my P's and Q's. And while it did require my constant effort and attention, in the end, the payoff was priceless. By winning the trust of the authority figures over me, I cast off the yoke of their suspicion, thereby gaining an incredible amount of freedom.

Yet despite my outward front, I lacked even the first ounce of integrity. Due to my lack of moral conviction, my actions rarely came into alignment with the motivation that lay just beneath the surface. And while the question of motives rarely came up, I trusted in my ability to throw out a canned answer and skirt by unnoticed. Since I didn't have to answer to God, I had no issue with lying straight-faced in order to maintain my cover.

Over time, this duplicity began to show up more and more in

different areas of my life. I was a smart kid and historically had no problem doing well in school. I knew that academic success was a doorway to all sorts of opportunity, so I always got my work done. But as my classes got harder toward the end of high school, I started looking for ways to cut corners and quickly discovered cheating to be much easier than I had originally thought.

My plan was never to stop studying, but simply to add cheating. To me, it was just an easy way to supplement my grades, two points here, five points there. And as I began to search out the opportunity to cheat, I seemed to find it in the most obvious places. Hidden notes and roaming eyes were my go-tos, and I dabbled in plagiarism as well. My school had a rigorous honor code, so I never cheated if I thought for a moment that I might get caught—yet when I saw an open door, I took it every time.

Cheating wasn't a necessity for me, but simply a way to work the system. I didn't cheat to pass high school. I cheated to make straight A's. I cheated to make the cum laude society. I cheated to get into a top ten university. Eventually, this way of thought became a way of habit and a way of life, so much so that by the time I got to college, I probably spent more time thinking up clever ways to avoid doing my work than I did actually studying.

The irony, of course, was the fact that I spent my senior year on the Honor Council to beef up my resume. I did not feel the slightest bit of remorse about this inconsistency, frankly because I had no concept of honor. The rules and regulations upheld by my school and other similar institutions did nothing in my eyes but limit my freedom for the sake of maintaining some obsolete moral standard.

As my double life permeated my existence more and more, it opened the door to a slew of other hidden vices. I spent a large amount of time looking at pornography and developed an entire skill set around finding it on the internet and hiding it in secret folders on our family computer. I was always one step ahead of my parents when it came to technology, so I didn't get caught but once or twice in all my years of living at home.

Even when I did get in trouble, I learned that I could talk myself out of pretty much anything. I always managed to come up with a good enough alibi to quell my parents' suspicions, adamantly insisting upon my innocence until they left me alone. As long as I got what I wanted in the end, nothing else really mattered to me.

This certainly applied to the owner of the restaurant that I stole from the summer after graduating from high school. My stealing was just as calculated as my cheating. I studied the systems and learned how to take a little here and a little there. I never stole more than fifteen or twenty dollars a day, yet rarely went a day without stealing. I even kept track on an Excel spreadsheet how much I earned in tips and how much I pocketed on the side.

My hidden life of deception slowly became a source of pride for me, and I gloated over the spotless image that I managed to maintain on the outside. In addition to making good grades, I coordinated volunteers for a tutoring program at the local Boys and Girls Club and helped out at the soup kitchen once a month. I went to church with my family every Sunday, attended youth group every Wednesday and helped out at several Christian youth retreats throughout my high school career. I even made Eagle Scout.

I had discovered that there were some very attractive girls at a particular church youth group in town and needed no further motivation to join. There the fact that I didn't hang out with the popular party crowd worked to my advantage, and I began to embrace a completely new identity.

Overnight, I joined the "straight edge" bandwagon, which to the other kids signified a commitment to abstain from alcohol and drugs. In my mind, it was just an easy way to fit in. Plus, it gave me an excuse to draw black X's on my hands and listen to heavy metal music at church.

Although my motives were not pure, being around good company did help me stay out of trouble. The first time I ever drank alcohol was junior year prom, and after that, I probably only drank a handful of times before leaving for college. I never smoked anything in high school, not even a single puff on a cigarette, and refused to even take aspirin or ibuprofen.

Yet deep down, I knew that it was a sham. The girls at youth group were the best option I had, and while I never once let on to any of my peers or adult leaders, they were the sole reason why I went week after week. Fortunately for me, though, everyone appeared to be satisfied by the simple fact that I showed up, and no one ever so much as asked me why I was there.

As long as I managed to fly under the radar, I thought everything would be just fine.

Chapter Two

Across The Desert

PARALYZED BY FEAR, my mind began to race uncontrollably. *Couldn't I have had this epiphany nine hours ago,* I thought to myself, *when I was still on solid ground? Now I'm going to die in the ocean! What an inconvenient place to hit rock bottom!*

As bad as things seemed, I knew that I had to do something. I flipped over onto my back, took a deep breath and started to reassess my situation. *Let's see. I'm in the middle of the ocean. I'm alone, naked and tired. There is no help in sight, and I've been out here longer than I really care to think about. Not ideal.*

What's more, I had been intentionally swimming hard all morning to tire myself out. Although I was not a regular swimmer, I did remember all of the strokes from summer swim team as a kid. I stuck mostly to breast stroke but threw in a few freestyle sprints along the way to expend extra energy. I even tried butterfly at one point. Let's just say that I had no intention of dragging the thing out.

Yet now with all of that swimming behind me, I realized what precious little strength I had remaining. I surely didn't have enough to dwell on the negatives, so I decided to focus on the one thing I still had going for me—I wasn't dead. The state of South Carolina may have its share of issues, but at least we have a great motto:

"Where there is breath, there is hope." *If I can somehow keep my head on my shoulders*, I thought, *I might actually find a way out of this mess.*

I surveyed the scene and noticed only two exceptions to the vast expanse of blue which surrounded me: the first, a single ship off in the distance and the second, a bright red buoy. Next, I lifted my body out of the water in hopes of spotting land. After a moment of searching, I located the shoreline and managed to reorient myself. I figured the beach to be due west, which meant that the ship was east and the little red buoy south.

I began to carefully consider these three possible directions. I figured that my chances of reaching the ship were slim to none, and since it would have taken me in the opposite direction of land anyway, I eliminated it as a possibility. While I longed to be back on dry ground, the buoy did look to be much closer than the beach, and if I were to reach it, I could just climb on and wait for a boat to rescue me. Even if it took a full day for someone to find me, I was ready to do anything to get out of that water.

As I started swimming toward the buoy, my excitement grew with the hope of finally getting a rest. I even pictured the newspaper headline: "Fishing Boat Rescues Naked Guy from Ocean Buoy." I know how deceptive gauging distances in the water can be, particularly from a low vantage point, but with positive thoughts beginning to run through my mind again, I convinced myself that the buoy was definitely getting closer.

The longer I swam, though, the more it became clear that this little red buoy stood farther away than it had initially appeared. I once again surveyed the scene and found myself in seemingly the same place I had started from, the boat and the buoy ultimately revealing themselves to be little more than a bunch of proverbial dangling grapes tantalizing me in the distance.

I knew that my energy had to be running low, so I gave up on chasing rabbits and did the only practical thing left—I swam toward land. Since I had a hard time seeing the beach from my position in the water, I decided to use the sun to guide me. I got the idea from a ridiculous movie called *In the Army Now*, where Pauly Shore used the sun to maintain his direction as he walked across the desert.

While I certainly did not expect to derive survival skills from a movie I saw one afternoon on daytime TV, the principle did make sense. I would orient myself toward land, notice the position of the sun and use it to keep me on track. I figured that if it worked in the desert, it would work in the ocean. So from that point on, I kept the sun out ahead to my left and was able to stay on course for the rest of my swim.

Well, almost the rest of my swim. Until I saw the jetties. *Jetties!* I thought. *I'm saved.* In fact, they looked so close that I felt like I could reach out and grab them. I immediately changed my course and began swimming in their direction. Yet as I headed toward the mysterious rock formation, I realized that much like the buoy, they did not appear to be getting any closer.

Then I thought about it for a moment. *Why would there be jetties in the middle of the ocean?* Jetties are man-made rock barriers used to protect harbors and inlets from ocean waves. Building them in the middle of open water would make absolutely no sense, not to mention that it would be flat-out impossible. This was clearly nothing more than a mirage, a sort of reverse oasis in my ocean desert.

Reluctantly, I turned from this false vision and started back on my previous course. Until, that is, I saw the second batch of jetties. *Jetties!* I rejoiced once again. *These look way too convincing not to be real.* Once again, I redirected my course and swam off toward the rocks. But as you may have guessed, they weren't real. And they weren't real the third time I swam toward them either. I finally resolved that this would be my last distraction and resumed my course toward the beach.

After that, I did the only sensible thing left to do. I swam. And I swam and I swam and I swam. I eventually reached the point where I could see the buildings on the shore, but for the most part, it felt like the more I swam, the more everything stayed in exactly the same place. *Shouldn't these buildings be getting bigger?* I tried not to pay any attention to this thought, since reaching land was truly my last hope, but deep down, I doubted if I would ever again stand on solid ground.

As the hours dragged on, I began to think more and more about my parents. My mother was 24 years old when she lost her sister in a car accident, and in many ways, the pain had never left. I desperately did not want to be another premature death for her to mourn, so I pressed on.

I fought with all of my being to keep hope alive and reassured myself that I must be getting closer. My energy level seemed to be holding steady, and I told myself that I would just have to stick it out until I got there. In fact, I was even starting to feel optimistic—then the sun began to set.

Dawn was just beginning to break when I entered the ocean that morning, and I watched the sunrise over the water from start to finish. So when the sky filled with streaks of orange and pink for the second time that day, I knew I was in deep trouble. I finally gained a concept of how long I had been in the water, and although I didn't rack my brain to count the hours, I knew it had been too long.

∞   HOPE AGAINST HOPE   ∞

WHEN GOVERNED BY a system of external authority, life revolves around rules and rewards. If a person does what is expected of them and behaves according to the established standard, they are rewarded, generally with some new aspect of personal freedom. If they break the rules, or rather if they are caught doing so, they are met with repercussions, thereby losing a certain amount of freedom.

Since I realized that my quality of life depended directly upon my level of individual freedom, I broke the rules with extreme caution. I paid close attention to the authority structure and always sought to exceed the expectations that were established for me. As a result of my spotless behavioral and academic record, I was allowed pretty much free reign, and the motives behind my actions never once came into question in all of my years living at home.

Not only did I slip undetected through the system at home and at school, but I managed to do it at church as well. All of my friends in the youth group appeared to be quite serious about the whole God thing, and although it didn't mean a lick to me, I went along with the program. I ate pizza when it was time to eat pizza, I mingled when it was time to mingle and I listened when it was time to listen. I even prayed out loud on occasion.

Over time, I got very used to putting on a show and doing everything right when others were around. My goal was to retain all of the rights and privileges gained by following the rules, while simultaneously possessing the freedom to act outside of all moral boundaries when no one was looking. In my mind, this duplicity epitomized freedom—to be an egoist in an altruistic world.

By definition, altruism is the quality of unselfish concern for the welfare of others. In an altruistic society, the community as a whole derives benefit from the sacrifice of the individual. Everyone helps everyone else, and no one seeks his own gain. Like an ant colony, the well-being of the community always trumps that of the individual, and the well-being of the individual hinges entirely upon the prosperity of the community as a whole.

Egoism, on the other hand, lies at the complete opposite end of the spectrum. In the mind of a pure egoist, not a single thought is wasted on ideals like the greater good or collective well-being. Each individual holds the responsibility to look out for himself, and the concept of self-sacrifice is utterly nonexistent. In an egoist society, greed and avarice rule the day.

Growing up in a Christian home, the behavioral standard set for me had always been based upon an altruistic set of values. And although the actions of those in authority over me didn't always look that way in practice, the ideal of other-mindedness was at very least championed. Service played a key role in day-to-day life, and the chief guiding principle seemed to be that if we all played by the rules, everything would work out just fine.

Since each individual living in an altruistic society benefits regardless of whether they uphold the ideals or not, my plan was to get the best of both worlds. While maintaining the guise of altruism, I would be a hidden egoist. Thus, I would be able to enjoy all of the advantages of living in a selfless community, with an added extra layer of benefit brought about by my secret, selfish actions.

Although I carefully followed all of the rules, I was rotten to the core. And since no one ever probed me on the motivation behind my actions, I passed right on through to high school graduation unnoticed. I often wonder what would have happened had someone ever challenged my motives. Would I have been sharp enough to deflect their inquisition, or would I have crumbled under the pressure, exposing my double life once and for all?

I will never know the answer to that question, and I do not believe in regret. I do know, however, that as soon as I got out from under the system of imposed boundaries and external restrictions, my life changed drastically. Once my parents dropped me off at college,

I discovered that my new world had very few rules and even fewer authority figures around to enforce them.

To my parents' credit, their rules served me well and protected me throughout my time living at home. But since I had already rejected the why behind the what—that is, the reason for the behavior rather than the behavior itself—life inside the lines was not sustainable for me outside of their system. I had played the game and passed with flying colors. I had earned the freedom to live on my own, and now I was going to give it a whirl.

Yet with new freedoms come new responsibilities. I attended a tough school and ended up with a particularly difficult course load my freshman year. I regularly went to class and tried my best to stay on top of my homework—not that I cared about the material. I just knew that as long as I posted decent grades and did my laundry and made that all-important phone call to Mom each and every Sunday, I would be more or less off the hook.

And of course, being five hours from home changed the game significantly. Suddenly, I had no one to monitor my behavior from day to day. The only authority figure in my world as far as I could tell was the hall RA, or "Resident Assistant." This guy was a grad student with twice as much work as any of us undergrads who received free housing in exchange for living amongst a hall full of freshmen.

Theoretically, he had the power to enforce campus policy and issue a write-up in the event he witnessed a rule violation. But on the second day of school, he called a hall meeting to inform us of his stringent enforcement policy, which went something like "what the RA doesn't see, doesn't happen." He went on to request that if we did decide to break the rules, to please keep our doors shut. That way, he wouldn't be liable.

I didn't wait long to exercise my new freedom. Within the first week of school, I made myself a fake ID and used it to buy over one hundred dollars worth of liquor from the local ABC store. I hid it under my bed on our completely dry freshman campus and started selling shots to other students in my dorm. I made weekly beer runs for my friends and always kept a small percentage as payment for my services.

I quickly began to adapt to the college party life. Thursday became the new Friday, and Wednesday the new Thursday. A clear consensus arose among my new friends about the purpose of our being at school, which matched my understanding exactly. Grades held value only in their ability to ensure tuition payments. Campus life, on the other hand, revolved around something totally different— having as much fun as possible.

Despite my expressed intention to maintain a relationship with a high school girlfriend, I hooked up with a new girl at one of the very first fraternity parties of the year. We started dating, and despite our both being virgins, she asked me if I'd like to have sex. I was a bit taken aback initially and told her that I needed some time to think about it. But after a few days, I realized that there was absolutely nothing stopping me.

I had been active in oral sex for years, and withholding any moral argument, there didn't appear to be any significant difference. Other than the fact that real sex could get her pregnant. She was already on the pill, though, so why not get some use out of it? That night, a week after we had first met, we began having unprotected sex and never looked back.

Right around that same time, I got my first tattoo—the word "hope" in script on my left thigh. Since I had no hope in God, I knew that I needed something bigger than myself to believe in. I speculated that perhaps there was still purpose to be found in this world, even without God, and that I simply had not found it yet.

So while I waited for that magical something to materialize, I clung to hope itself.

I once heard about a science experiment that well illustrates the necessity of hope. First, a Plexiglas container is filled with water. A platform is moved next to the container at water lever, but it is kept on the outside. A live rat is then dropped into the water. For hours, the rat swims in circles, desperately trying to make its way onto the platform. But since the solid ground is unreachable, the rat eventually becomes exhausted and drowns.

Next, the same container is filled with the same amount of water and placed alone on a table, this time without the platform. A second live rat is dropped into the water. The rat swims two laps around the outside of the container, ducks its head under the water and sinks to the bottom where it drowns instantly. Now that's science for you.

Although the experiment is a bit morbid, it does illustrate a point. As soon as the rat discovered that there was no hope, it died. Life is impossible without something to live for—and I simply was not ready to duck my head under just yet.

∞ OUTSIDE LOOKING IN ∞

WHILE I CERTAINLY CUT LOOSE freshman year, college life had a much tamer side to it as well. Video games and pickup basketball occupied a large portion of my time, and I even joined the men's volleyball team. On Saturdays, my friends and I would trek across campus to watch our notoriously bad football team get trounced by some conference rival. At least the hotdogs were good.

Our basketball team, on the other hand, was a whole different story, and a tangible fervor swept the campus throughout the entire season. Eager to be in the center of the action, a group of my freshman classmates and I camped out over the course of six weeks to claim the front row at several of the games. One guy even returned to school three days before second semester classes began and slept alone in his tent until reinforcements arrived.

One of our primary responsibilities as diehard fans was to think up clever cheers, which we periodically chose to express via body paint. On one such occasion, our group came up with what we thought to be a particularly witty slogan and all pitched in on a couple buckets of paint. We assigned everyone a letter, including two spaces and an exclamation mark, and proceeded to coat ourselves despite the January cold.

Some of us also painted our hair, and when my turn came, I decided for the sake of time to dump half a can of blue paint on my head. We won the game and left the arena in high spirits, only to discover upon returning to our dorms that the paint wasn't coming off. As it turns out, rather than buying latex *body* paint, we purchased latex *house* paint—which carried with it a guarantee to last for at least ten years.

Although my coat didn't last quite that long, my girlfriend and I found ourselves picking blue paint out of my hair for the next two weeks. I thought it was a lot cooler than she did and actually enjoyed my new fashion statement. I had always been a big fan of the movie *SLC Punk*, which featured Matthew Lillard rocking bright blue hair, plus I really just liked the attention.

Until, that is, I got cut from the fraternity I had set my sights on from the beginning of the year. One of the more exclusive groups on campus, I knew that a bid from them would immediately boost me up the social ladder. While I was enjoying all of the other aspects of school life, I had entered college with a very specific set of motives. I realized that I would have a fresh start there and resolved to build myself an entirely new reputation.

Throughout my high school career, I remained bitter over the fact that I had never been given a chance and felt that my social potential had suffered greatly from my poor reception in the sixth grade. This was my opportunity to be the person I had always wanted to be—and to prove to everyone that I had what it took to be popular.

The way I saw it, there was no doubt that Greek life held the greatest potential for immediate social advancement. Since my school had a second semester rush, my friends and I spent the first half of the year going to as many frat parties as possible. There were two major benefits to this system: the first being free alcohol and the second, an opportunity to impress the upperclassmen.

Once rush officially started, my plan was just to stay cool and lay low. I thought that if I could blend in and avoid doing anything really stupid, I would be able to glide my way right on through. This turned out to be easier than I had expected, since it appeared that the only requirement for acceptance was to show up and drink a lot. That I could handle.

As the series of rush events continued, all seemed to be going as planned. I continued to meet more of the brothers at each new function and maintained perfect attendance. Plus, I quickly found out that I could drink a whole lot more than I ever imagined, which turned out to be a major asset during rush. For a brief moment in time, I felt like I was on top of the world.

This of course made it all the more difficult for me when I got cut after the second round. Completely devastated, I racked my brain for a reason why I had been weeded out. I went to all of the events and did everything required of me, if not more. I showed up when it was time to show up, I drank when it was time to drink and I schmoozed when it was time to schmooze. What else could they possibly want from me?

As I lay in my bed later that night picking blue paint from my head, I zeroed in on the only possible explanation—it must have been the hair. The fraternity was of the traditional "Old South" order, and ever since the paint incident, I had felt a bit out of place. They must have written me off as a member of the "alternative" crowd, which didn't really jibe stylistically with bow ties and seersucker suits. I could not believe I had made such a stupid mistake.

Immediately, I began to experience the same feeling of rejection that I had felt over seven years before. I found myself once again on the outside of the exclusive club that I longed to be a part of, this time with no hope of ever breaking in. This fraternity was supposed to be my ticket to a better life, and I had been waiting for years to cash in. Now my spirit had once more been deflated, and I felt utterly lost.

Despite my inner turmoil, I knew exactly how to respond. Since appearances were everything to me, I figured that I could just change my tune and still manage to come out smelling rosy. All at once, I hopped on the anti-Greek bandwagon and started espousing the negative externalities of this elitist and antiquated system. I told myself and others how I refused to be confined to one exclusive clique and how much better off I was on my own.

I'll show them how to have a good time.

∞ THE REST OF MY LIFE ∞

FOLLOWING THIS NEW REJECTION, I began to significantly alter the course my life. I latched closely onto my girlfriend and became increasingly intrigued by the thought of illegal drugs. I had never taken any drugs up to this point, aside from cough medicine and the occasional antibiotic, and I really didn't even know where to start. But as fate would have it, my girlfriend was light-years ahead of me on the experimental side, so I ended up just stealing my drugs from her.

I was forced to steal them because, up to this point, I had been so obnoxious about telling her how "straight edge" I was that she refused to share them with me. It had been such a part of my identity in high school that I naturally carried it into college. And although I had long since broken down the alcohol barrier, I remained very proud of the fact that I had never taken any drugs or even smoked a single cigarette.

But all of that changed one night when I took a quarter ounce of hallucinogenic mushrooms from my girlfriend's stash. I ate them alone in my room and soon became incoherent. Since I couldn't let her find out about my trip, I decided to leave the dorm until the effects wore off. I walked until I reached the edge of campus where I found a grassy field, and I took a seat underneath a grove of massive oak trees.

Despite the secrecy of my excursion, I greatly enjoyed the effects that the drugs were having on my mind. I found myself in a state of utter contentment simply rubbing my hands back and forth over the grass. I marveled at how beautiful the trees were and noticed all of the very interesting details of my new environment. I found a gazebo nearby next to a life-sized statue of a man and proceeded to converse with him for quite some time.

Every hour or so, I would start walking back to my dorm, only to remember that I was still high as a kite and in no condition to be speaking with anyone. So I would just sit back down in the grass or walk over to visit with the statue some more. I had plenty of time to think about my predicament and began to realize that I had entirely misunderstood the essence of the drug trip.

For years, I thought that "tripping" was a particular feeling one got from taking drugs, which would alter one's perception of reality for a short time. I imagined a world full of strange colors and psychedelic music and hippies dancing around in tie-dye shirts. Perhaps one would even be so fortunate as to see a real live hallucination, like a leprechaun or the Easter Bunny.

Yet as I sat in the field that night, I realized that tripping is not so much a sensation as it is a journey, like boarding a nonstop train. As soon as the doors close behind you and the train begins to move, it's best to let go of all frivolous thoughts of deboarding and to simply prepare yourself for the ride. At this point, the only way to get off the train is to wait for it to come to a halt.

In the same way, once a drug has been ingested, the exit doors slam shut. The train starts picking up steam, and the ride begins. What happens on the train might be trippy, but then again it might not be. That's not really the point. The key is the journey, or the trip itself. And while to some this might seem like a frivolous distinction, to me, it was one of those rare moments of grand revelation.

Life is a trip, I thought to myself. *We're all on this train together.* Suddenly, my world became crystal clear. Reality, consciousness, human existence—everything—it all made sense. I had uncovered the meaning of life, the ultimate purpose of man, and the way I would spend the rest of my time on earth, all in one fell swoop. I pondered my new discovery all night, and by the time I returned to my dorm room, I was ecstatic.

I rushed to my computer and began to record this new revelation. Due to a strong distaste for MS Word autocorrect, I opened up Notepad and hammered out my manifesto in a matter of minutes. Entitled "the rest of my life," I envisioned this document serving as the guiding force of my entire existence, the foundation on which I would base all of my major life decisions from that point on. I have included it here in its non-corrected entirety.

the rest of my life.txt

i have the answer
the key to life
one big wink of an eye
sticking its tongue out at us
its all a joke
just one big joke
thats why we're all here
thats why we choose the strong ones (to play with us)
so just smile
thats what hes doing
thats what shes doing
enjoy it
this is what billions of years have produced
this feeling
this coolness
so stop hating
stop being jealous
because you are him
YOU ARE HIM - THE ONE THAT YOU'VE ALWAYS WANTED TO BE
so apreciate those among us
appreciate the players among us
you've got 50 billion how about 60
im still laughing at you
WE ARE STILL LAUGHING AT YOU
it all makes sense now
dont go back to the way it was
HATS OFF TO THE PLAYERS AMONG US
ALWAYS SMILING
WE'RE GOING TO MAKE IT EASY FOR EACH OTHER
WE ARE THAT PERSON
ENLIGHTENMENT
ENLIGHTENMENT
I HAVE ENLIGHTENED MYSELF
i get IT
because the night belongs to us
because i cant get fired
i am joining the fight
i have had my last doubt
my last doubt - JULY 15th - 16th -

```
how bout the 17th
the 18th - the 19th
why does it matter?
i am above the struggle
i am on top
WE ARE ON TOP
so dont let it wind down
yeah we do yeah we do
free your mind
let it go
let it go
happiness is here
just get on board
and thank the (lord)...
DONT HATE
stop fighting and just let it ride
and i am passionate about that
you make the rules
and we will get around them
and then we'll stick our tongues out at you

i still dont know what comes next
but ive decided to stop worrying about it
```

When I awoke the next morning, the train had come to a complete stop, and I found myself back in the same old normal world that I had spent my entire life in. Yet I refused to let go of my experience and remained utterly convinced that the drugs had opened new doors of perception. I had seen the truth—that life was nothing more than one big cosmic joke—and I could not wait to share my discovery with the world.

I honestly believed that I had unearthed something monumental and decided to pursue it with all of my being. I would show everyone once and for all that I possessed the capacity for greatness. I had found my ultimate purpose and was prepared to set my course.

Little did I know that I was headed directly toward the Atlantic Ocean.

∞ NOTHING TO LOSE ∞

AS MY DRUG USE INCREASED over the following weeks and months, so did my confidence in my newfound philosophical direction. I spent the summer in Charleston working at a restaurant by day and partying by night, after which I returned to school for my sophomore year. By this time, I was ready to make a permanent statement about my beliefs and decided on two additional tattoos that would visually represent unwavering commitment to the defining principles of my life.

The first of these tattoos, and my second overall, was a solid green star on the inside of my right wrist. It served as a constant reminder to live life to the fullest every single day, as well as a self-sabotage safeguard against ever entering corporate America. Since I believed that death would be the end of all consciousness, I decided to spend the tiny sliver of time I had left on this earth maximizing physical pleasure at every opportunity. I was going to live like, pardon the cliché of my 19-year-old mind, a rock star.

Well, at least a rock star that went to most of his classes. Even though my heart's desire was to throw all caution to the wind, I realized that there still remained an aspect of external restriction on my life, namely from my parents. Because despite the fact that they lived 300 miles away, they were still my sole source of income. And since a certain grade level was expected in order for them to continue paying tuition, my quality of life directly hinged on my performance in the classroom.

So while I couldn't have cared less about my schoolwork, I did perceive that the next three years of my life had the potential to be pretty doggone swell—if I kept my grades up, that is. I resolved to exert just enough effort to get by, basically as little work as humanly possible, and to spend the remainder of my time partying.

At this point, my reasoning seemed perfectly logical. The only alternative in my mind was to follow in the footsteps of my parents toward a life of hard work and sacrifice, and I simply did not see the value in it. Sure, we had a nice family—we lived in a nice house, wore nice clothes and drove around in nice cars. We even belonged to the country club.

Yet through the lens of my Godless worldview, none of those things had any bearing on my ultimate reality or the ultimate reality of anyone else. In light of eternity, the "good life" that my parents had established for themselves was no better and no worse than any lifestyle I might happen to choose for myself. All of the country clubs in the world couldn't change the fact that we were both going to die and rot in the ground like everyone else on the planet.

I believed that I had absolutely nothing to lose and saw no sense in working hard to attain happiness, particularly since my "shortcut" methods—drugs, alcohol, sex, pornography and gambling to name a few—seemed to work just fine. What began as a rejection of the traditional models of success had morphed into a complete dismissal of any and all moral grounding. As Friedrich Nietzsche put it, "If God is dead, then everything is permitted."

My life soon degenerated into a hedonistic quest for instant gratification. If it felt good, I did it. If not, I avoided it like the plague—regardless of what "it" was. Deep down, I knew that this lifestyle was not beneficial or sustainable, yet I championed it and even advocated it to others nonetheless.

Since I defined freedom in my mind as simply the absence of all commitment, I was a real snake to the women in my life. While I had no problem saying whatever it took to get a girl in bed, I refused to provide any assurance of security in my relationships. Because you never know when someone more attractive might come along. If the girl of my dreams were to walk into my life tomorrow, I needed to be ready. I wasn't about to miss that kind of opportunity on account of some chick I happened to be sleeping with today.

No, I refused to spend the best years of my life tied down. I believed that the pinnacle of human existence lay in the ability to do whatever I wanted, whenever I wanted. I recognized no authority in my life and allowed no one to tell me what to do; well, no one other than those who carried guns and had the power to throw me into a prison cell. I listened to them and obeyed in the public sphere, but that was about the extent of it.

I saw no merit in their rules, the laws of the land, and at the end of the day I really just wanted to be left alone to pursue happiness on my own terms. *Isn't that the essence of the American Dream?* I thought. *Life and liberty and all that jazz. My parents were allowed to seek happiness through career and family—why shouldn't I be allotted the same freedom, to seek it through drugs and sex?*

If only they could see how good these things made me feel, then they would understand. Isn't that the bottom line after all, to feel good? Why else would my parents spend their time raising a family and going on vacation and playing sports and eating giant tubs of popcorn at the movies? Aren't we all essentially after the same end?

Sure, I understood that my lifestyle was less sustainable than that of my parents. They were hoping to live well beyond eighty, while I had no intention of ever reaching thirty. But what's eighty years in light of eternity? The answer, of course, is exactly the same as twenty. Or thirty. Or any finite number. *How could they not see,* I wondered, *that our lives mean nothing?*

I, on the other hand, did see and vowed not to let their ignorance hold me back any longer. I refused to go through life like just another dull star in the night sky, shining slow and steady for years and years, indistinguishable from all of the others, only to one day drop unnoticeably out of existence. No, I wanted to sparkle and fade, to be a shooting star that everyone would see, even if it lasted only for a single moment.

In a flash of glory, I would streak across the sky—and then simply be done with it.

∞ DOWN THE RABBIT HOLE ∞

IF MY STAR TATTOO had set my course, then it was my third—a white rabbit on the inside of my left heel—that powered the ship. This image carries a strong drug connotation in American culture and has ever since the late 1960s, when the band Jefferson Airplane wrote a song connecting Lewis Carol's imagery from *Alice in Wonderland* to the hallucinatory effects of psychedelic drugs.

Since I basically thought that drugs were the best thing since sliced bread, as well as a major key to living a pleasure-filled life, my rabbit tattoo was first and foremost a symbol of my dedication. The irony was that while I flat out refused to acknowledge even the smallest semblance of commitment in my dating relationships, I had no trouble showcasing my passionate loyalty to drug use itself.

In addition to the simple pleasure I derived from them, I also believed that drugs contained the power to unlock doors of perception in the mind, leading to new levels of thinking and even to parallel realms of existence. Thus, a major element of the tattoo's symbolism was wrapped up in my quest for personal enlightenment, my search for the elusive rabbit hole that would take me into a new echelon of reality.

During the time since my first mushroom trip, I had observed a disconnect between the beauty of nature and the cruelty of the human race, concluding that this world could not possibly be the final manifestation of our creation. But since I did not believe in life after death, I imagined that perhaps there was a better place hidden somewhere here on this side of the grave—essentially like heaven on earth—a place I simply referred to as "Wonderland."

And although I was not sure that this theoretical place even existed, I really didn't have much else going for me and decided to pursue it wholeheartedly. Since I believed that drugs were my only hope of ever finding this blissful realm, I adopted a new personal drug policy. Whenever I met someone who had drugs of any kind, I would buy as much as they would agree to sell, right then and there.

I never passed up an opportunity to try a new drug and started paying close attention to the effects they had on my body and mind. I figured that I would just take as many drugs as I could for as long as possible and then see what happened. Since I had no other tangible goals to strive for, I embraced this as a challenge and began to view myself as sort of a walking, talking drug experiment.

While hallucinogens had always held a special place in my heart, pot soon became my drug of choice simply due to its widespread availability. Even when traveling, I could typically score at least a joint's worth inside of 24 hours, and by the end of my sophomore year, smoking weed had become a daily routine. Over time, I learned how to make a bong out of just about anything and could practically roll a joint in my sleep. I smoked out of beer cans, soda bottles, orange juice cartons and even plastic BIC pens. I was like the pothead version of MacGyver.

During this time in my life, it would have been a rare occasion for me not to have drugs of some kind on my person. If it wasn't my little baggie of weed, it may have been coke or ecstasy or a pain pill.

My two best friends and I split an ounce of pot every two weeks, which was enough to keep me high for a good portion of the time. If one of us hadn't finished his stash before the new stuff came in, we would just roll a couple of massive joints and then start all over again.

I honestly had no clue how dependent I was until I tried to quit once. I didn't have a good reason—just my own curiosity to see if I could do it. I picked a day for the experiment and managed to stave off the temptation for about three miserable hours. Then I broke down and took a hit from the household gravity bong. I decided later that my attempt had been pretty pathetic, so I tried again the next day and caved after just thirty minutes.

Although my quest for freedom and enlightenment had led me into drug use from the start, here I found myself in fetters once again. Rather than being bound by the rules of my parents' generation, I had become reliant upon drugs. Yet I had way too much invested in this thing to turn back so quickly, and as long as I had enough pot, my world was peachy keen. In the end, I simply accepted that this is how it would always be, until I died or couldn't afford to buy drugs anymore.

Over time, I grew increasingly more apathetic toward life in general. The more I smoked, the more disconnected from reality I became. As a sophomore, I remember going to a Goldman Sachs interview for a summer internship position and telling the recruiters that my greatest weakness was my inability to wake up to my alarm in the morning. Needless to say, they didn't call me back for the second round.

While I did like the idea of making a lot of money—drugs cost money—I knew all too well that a demanding job on Wall Street would never suit. I wanted something where I wouldn't have to work so hard, which is precisely why I took to gambling. I realized that the odds at a casino or for the lottery would always be against me, but I had heard that poker was a good way to make easy money. I began to search out games on campus, ones with high enough stakes to be worth my time, and played as often as I could.

I had grown up playing cards—bridge, hearts, spades, gin rummy, you name it—and found that I had a knack for poker from the get-go. In fact, the more I played, the more money-making potential I saw. I read books on poker and became an avid student of the game. In addition to the live tables on campus, I started playing online as well and spent hours a day glued to my computer screen with rapt attention. I would often stay up all night long, stopping occasionally to blink, with the dream of making it big.

Yet at the very same time, my parents were paying forty thousand dollars a year for me to attend one of the top universities in the world. Blind to the irony of the situation, I had no concept of the opportunity that I so casually threw away each day. Looking back, I would probably have a law degree if I had spent half as much time studying as I did playing poker.

Eventually, I developed an addiction to gambling which may have even rivaled my drug habit. I spent the first semester of my junior year studying abroad in Sydney, Australia and began making frequent trips to the casino downtown with a close friend. No matter how hard we tried, regardless of what time limit we set for ourselves, we always stayed until they shut the place down at 4 a.m.

Throughout the semester, a roommate of mine regularly invited me to go surfing, yet I never once took him up on it. This was largely due to the fact that on most days, I went to bed around the time he got up. He did finally convince me to go on a weekend surf trip with him, but since I was more interested in smoking pot with the locals, I ended up spending very little time in the water.

In fact, the highlight of my surf weekend was meeting a guy who agreed to sell me some ecstasy. He had a connection back in Sydney, so I told him to buy as much as he could. We then agreed to meet up at his place in a few weeks to make the exchange. My total came to 350 dollars—my largest drug transaction to date—but since I was doing well at the card table, I didn't give it a second thought.

The gambling and the drugs complemented each other well in my mind, and I started feeling like a real big shot. I caught the glimmer of potential for major gain and had no qualms about betting hundreds of dollars on a roll of the dice. I even occasionally ventured into thousand-dollar poker games online, with the hope of hitting the jackpot for real.

I felt completely untouchable, as if nothing in this world could bring me down. When I returned to the states from Australia, my illusion of invincibility reached the point that I flew from Sydney to Los Angeles to Charleston with two hits of ecstasy in my pocket. I had no fear of being caught and even engaged an official at the airport about the best way to transport drugs internationally. I concluded our conversation by informing him that if it were me, I would simply carry them on my person.

It may have been risky, but at least it got my adrenaline going.

CHAPTER THREE

DEAD MAN WALKING

AS DARKNESS BEGAN TO SETTLE upon the water, I found myself unable to swim another stroke. Like a noose tightening around my neck, I could feel the fast-approaching night maliciously crushing all hope of survival. I turned over onto my back, thrusting my chin high into the air to avoid the ocean spray, and found myself almost unintentionally crying out for help.

In my rational mind, I knew that the attempt was futile—still it made no difference. A deep and powerful animal instinct had seemingly grabbed hold of my body, causing it to roar forth with every fiber of my being. With back arched, arms wide and fists clenched, I strained each muscle from head to toe, almost as if to battle the impending doom directly.

"Help!" I shouted with all of my strength. "Help!!!" Again and again I cried out, keeping nothing back, emptying myself on each successive howl.

"HELP!!!"

My monosyllabic plea grew louder and longer until I reached the point of exhaustion and could sound off no more. The tension immediately fled from my wasted body, and with a tiny inkling of hope, I tuned my ear for a reply. Yet the ocean offered none.

Slowly, I drifted along in silent desperation. I began to see in my mind's eye all of the bridges I had burned to get to this place of isolation, remembering the countless people I had turned away and all of the helping hands I had rejected, each one with the potential to be the lifeline that could have ultimately saved me from this grim fate.

One of those lifelines had actually come during my swim, in the form of a Coast Guard boat. Half an hour after I had left the beach, the boat passed by no more than 100 feet away from me. Of course at that time, I did not want to be found, so I ducked my head under the water and hoped that they would just pass on by. Sure enough, they failed to spot me, and I never saw them again. *What I wouldn't do for that boat right now!*

Somehow out of my disconsolate state, I mustered up the strength to cry out one last time, as if pleading with the ocean herself to extend an arm of mercy and spare my life. Once again, though, the water only taunted me with silence. *You're on your own, pal*, it whispered coldly. I desperately wanted to lash out in anger against this cruel and unfeeling force that held me captive, yet deep down I knew that I had no grounds for offense. I had chosen my fate, and it was mine alone to bear.

My arms felt like two lead weights as my long day in the water finally caught up with me. I once again fought against the impending despair and attempted to resume swimming, only this time my strokes lacked confidence. I could feel the fear building inside of me and watched intently as the light rays grew longer and dimmer, until one by one they vanished below the horizon.

As the colors from the sunset faded, darkness descended upon me like a shroud slowly covering my world. I could feel my body as it started to sink, and for a moment, I slipped beneath the inky surface of the sea. I called on my last ounce of strength and fought to bring my head above the water, gasping frantically for breath. The sea suddenly had a new quality, a sinister look to it, as the murky water chopped up and down. I watched helplessly as my remaining sliver of hope disappeared with the final strands of daylight.

Too tired to continue and with nowhere else to turn, I did the only thing left to do. I prayed to God. To be honest, I really don't know why it came to mind at all. Apart from my recent Messiah complex, God had played no part in my life for several years leading up to this point. I wasn't even sure if God existed. And if he did, why would he help someone like me who had ignored him for so long?

In the end, though, I had nothing to lose and no other option. So while floating on my back, I offered up my last-ditch effort at survival and prayed to God for the first time in years. Since I didn't know what to say, I just blurted out the first thing that came to mind, promising God that if he delivered me to land safely, I would never drink alcohol or take drugs again as long as I lived.

I also added that I would never smoke cigarettes again because I figured if you're going to get rid of vices, you might as well kick them all at once. Lastly, I made a single caveat to allow for prescription drugs as long as they were prescribed to me. I could just imagine telling my doctor that I wouldn't be able to take the blood pressure meds he was recommending because of a deal I had made with God in the ocean.

The moment I finished praying, I saw a group of white birds fly overhead, which I took as a sign that God had heard my plea, and I decided to press on. I quickly found that the only way for me to continue was by hyperventilating, so I began huffing and puffing just to keep my head above the water's surface. As the night wore on, I noticed more and more illuminated buildings on the beach ahead, and since I no longer had the sun to keep me on course, I picked one to use as my spot.

For the rest of the night, I alternated swimming ten counts of breast stroke on my stomach, followed by ten counts on my back, just kicking to give my arms a rest. Then I would repeat. Several times after finishing a count on my back, I would flip over to find that I had been going in the completely wrong direction. Yet as frustrating as it may have been, I had no other option but to simply turn around and keep swimming.

As I drew nearer to shore, the ocean waves became a major hazard, particularly during the stints on my back. Unable to see them coming or anticipate their frequency, I was afforded no opportunity to brace myself until the waves were already crashing over my head. This coupled with my rapid breathing caused me to swallow, and aspirate, a large amount of ocean water.

While the battle inside of my physical body raged on, I found myself locked in a mental struggle as well. In order to find the will to keep going, I imagined myself playing in the waning minutes of a basketball game. I dug deep in search of the hidden energy reservoir that had served as my last line of defense so many times in the past. Despite the fact that my body was running on empty, I pressed on and reminded myself that I had never once given up before the final buzzer sounded.

Eventually, the second half ended in my mind, and the game moved into overtime. Although the light from the buildings seemed to linger at an incredible distance, I would periodically plunge down with my big toe in an attempt to find the ocean floor—but to no avail. As I swam and swam, the first overtime turned into the second, and the second into the third. Weary, worn and completely out of steam, I expected each count to be my last.

Afraid I could go no further, I probed the depth one last time for solid ground. My foot struck bottom. *Did I just feel sand?* With mind reeling, I thrust both legs underneath me, only to discover that I was standing chest deep in the water. *Land ho!* I could not believe what was happening. I felt like leaping for joy. But since I was still a considerable distance from shore, I knew that I was not completely out of Dodge. I fixed my gaze on the shoreline ahead and slowly made my way through the breaking waves toward the beach.

When I had passed the surf, I ran forward about three steps and collapsed on the sandy ground, as if to hug the sweet earth that had received me back into her arms. I realized after a few seconds, though, that lying on the beach was not getting me any closer to finding help, so I hoisted myself up and began walking toward the building directly before me.

Still in survival mode, I focused on putting one foot in front of the other. I noticed that while my arms felt like Jello, my legs were actually in pretty good shape. I decided that it must be due to the fact that I don't kick properly when I swim, and just as I was making a mental note to work on my form—wham! I fell headlong into the brush just in front of the sand dunes. Apparently, I had made it to the top of the beach.

I sat naked and tangled in the vegetation for a moment before attempting to stand again. *As if I didn't feel pathetic enough already.* Although the building stood a mere fifty yards in front of me, there appeared to be no beach access. Since I didn't have any pride left to lose, I hoisted myself up and started walking down the beach in search of a boardwalk.

Due to the hours of hyperventilating in the water, my breathing remained shallow, and I felt a constant dull pain lingering in my chest. Every minute or so, I would accidentally breathe too deeply, causing my lungs to sting sharply. As a result, I was only able to draw small, quick breaths and found myself half-panting to get enough oxygen.

Yet despite the pain, I felt an even stronger sensation rising up inside of me, which can only be described as unbridled joy. After all was said and done, I had two very exciting things going for me. First, I was on land. Second, I could walk. Then it hit me. *I'm on land. And I can walk. I'm alive!*

I had made it. I was a dead man walking.

∞ LOOK IN THE MIRROR ∞

THE MONTH IS JANUARY 2005. I awake to find myself in a room I've never seen before. Due to a severe hangover, it's painful to lift my head, but I do it anyway in order to take a look around. I don't recognize the decor, yet quickly realize that I'm in a dorm room on campus. I am lying on a futon that has been folded out in the middle of the room, occupying the majority of the floor space. The sunlight streaming full force through the windows tells me that it's not early. So much for going to class.

Although I have no recollection of how I got here, I do have a vague impression from the night before to work with. For starters, I know that I began drinking early in the evening at my apartment a mile or so off campus. I poured Southern Comfort into a 16.9 oz water bottle and drank the entire thing over the course of about an hour while my friends and I played beer pong.

Next, I remember being driven to a bar downtown. Once we got there, though, the only memory I have came from early in the night, when I lost my balance hugging a girl I barely knew. We ended up on the floor together for just a moment, and I have a vivid picture of staring up at the ceiling. Then nothing. *How did I get to campus?* I wondered. *Why didn't someone just take me home?*

As I'm recalling these events, the door swings open, and a girl enters the room. She is a year behind me in college, but we are from the same home town and know each other from high school. Dressed for class and wearing a bookbag, she begins searching for something on her desk. She finds what she is looking for and turns to leave the room, noticing for the first time that I am awake. I catch her eye but am still too dazed to say anything. After a brief moment, she breaks the silence. "You need to look in the mirror, Matt."

Her tone is harsh, and I am a bit taken aback. I've never heard her speak to me like this before. *Good morning to you, too*, I think sarcastically. But the last thing I want to do is seem ungrateful for her hospitality, and since I still don't have a grasp on what happened the night previous, I decide to go with a more neutral approach to ease the tension. "Is this your room?" I asked.

She pauses for a moment, turns toward me and puts her hand on her hip as if she has something to say. In the end, though, she must have decided that it wasn't worth her time because after a brief sigh, she only repeats her original statement, this time in a much gentler tone. "You need to look in the mirror, Matt." She then leaves the room.

Alone again, I let my head drop back on the pillow. I begin racking my brain to see if I can remember what stupid thing I may have done the night before to make her angry at me. Yet it feels as if there is a wall standing between my conscious state and my memory, and I continue to draw a blank. Painfully, I work my way out of bed, stretch for a brief moment and walk over to the full length mirror hanging on the wall by the door. It doesn't take long to realize what she meant—my entire face is covered with blood.

I can hardly believe my eyes and immediately begin to examine myself. I have never been in a fight in my whole life, so I cannot imagine that being the case. I wash off all the dried blood and find cuts on my forehead, nose and left cheek bone. It looks like I got in a fight with the pavement and lost.

I learned later that when my friend found me, I had been leaning up against a light post, bleeding from the face. Seeing as how I was completely incoherent, she kindly helped me back to her room and offered me her futon.

While I was certainly thankful for her hospitality, I still could not understand why she had been so stern. *Nights like these come with the territory of a good party*, I thought. *What's the big deal? Maybe she's just mad that I got blood on her pillow case.*

Yeah, that's probably it.

∞ SEARCHING FOR SIGNS ∞

AS THE SEMESTER PROGRESSED, my already failing grasp of reality started to slip more and more. Despite my initial resolve to do enough work to appease my parents, I stopped exerting any effort, and my grades began to plummet. I lost all sight of the future and turned a corner in my decision-making, which became a function with only one variable—how I felt at the moment. *I'm too smart to fail out of school*, I thought, *even without going to class.*

A month or so before the end of the semester, I sprained my ankle playing basketball. My class attendance was sparse enough already, but having to walk around on crutches pushed me over the edge. I finally gave up on school altogether and devoted two weeks toward the singular pursuit of reaching what I called "the next level of high," deciding to smoke pot on the hour every hour to see just how stoned I could get.

I had read that the active ingredient in marijuana, THC, stays in your body for quite some time after smoking. So unlike alcohol tolerance, where your body needs more and more to get drunk, pot works in the opposite way; the high actually builds as the THC levels in your body increase. Speculating that this might be my portal to Wonderland, I set out to discover a whole new sphere of marijuana-high.

One afternoon about a week later, I awoke in my room to a strange sound, similar to that of ocean waves crashing on the beach. It seemed to be increasing in volume, and as I listened closely, I began to hear a single word emerging from out of the noise—the word "peace." I quickly jumped out of bed to check my computer, but it sat silent. And since I was alone in the apartment, I could not imagine where the sound might be coming from.

After ruling out all other possibilities, I decided that it must be in my head. I had never experienced anything quite like this and wondered if it might be supernatural. One of the main ideas behind my "hope" tattoo was that while I didn't believe in God at the time, I did desire to maintain a hope that he might reveal himself to me one day. *Could today be the day?*

Looking for a sign of confirmation, I opened up iTunes just to see what would come up. I shuffled randomly forward, and the first song that appeared was "War" by System of a Down. *Interesting*, I thought. *Exactly the opposite of peace.* I listened for a moment and then shuffled forward again, this time landing on "One Tin Soldier" by Joan Baez. As the track started to play, my eyes instantly teared up. It was a song I knew well from summer camp as a child.

The song tells the story of two groups of people who go to battle over a treasure that is buried on a mountainside. After much carnage and bloodshed, a victor finally emerges. Yet when they go to unearth their sought-after treasure, they find only the words "peace on earth" written beneath—words that close out the final verse.

It's a sign!

As I reflected on the potential meaning of this occurrence, I was taken back to the three evidences of the eternal that I had discovered as a child. Although I had been a self-proclaimed atheist for nearly two years leading up to this point, I once again opened my mind to the possibility of God's existence and began searching for signs of life in the spiritual realm.

Yet after two full weeks of my pot experiment, I had reached no further breakthrough. The highs had long since leveled out, and my days were beginning to seriously blur together. Plus, no matter how hard I tried, I could not reproduce the sound of peace that had descended upon me. I knew that if I was going to find Wonderland, I would need something a whole lot stronger than pot.

Not long after, my best friend at school informed me of a dealer he knew in his home town who could allegedly get me any drug I wanted. I had been trying for some time to get my hands on a more powerful hallucinogen than mushrooms, either mescaline or LSD, yet due to the waning popularity of these types of drugs, my attempts thus far had been futile. Needless to say, my interests were piqued, and although I was given no guarantee, the simple prospect proved to be ample motivation for me to book a plane ticket.

The only dates my friend and I could work out for my visit fell during a week that my father had planned to take my brother and me hiking in the Grand Canyon. I didn't want to bail on my family, but I also was not about to pass up an opportunity to land LSD. I finally told my dad that my ankle was still too sore to do any hiking, and while there may have been a hint of truth to that statement, let's just say that I did not take crutches with me on my trip.

A week later, thanks to the easiest course load I could manage and some serious over-the-shoulder help on an Econ final, I passed the semester at school. This meant bottom line that I was off the hook for the summer, so I packed up my things and headed home to

Charleston. I spent a few days there putting on my best face for my parents and then took off to see about some drugs.

When I arrived at the airport, my friend greeted me with good news. Not only did he have some top notch bud for us, his dealer had scored thirty hits of acid. *Thirty hits of acid!* I almost lost it right there in the airport. I could barely contain my excitement the whole way to his house and just kept bouncing the idea off the walls of my mind. *Thirty hits of acid. Wonderland, here I come!*

∞   THE PROCESS OF DELUSION   ∞

THE HUMAN MIND IS a mysterious place. It is with the mind that a person is able to justify anything—any thought, decision or action—regardless of how heinous. What unfathomable amounts of injustice and evil have been perpetrated throughout history by those fully convinced of their own rightness? Yet it is always the same. We set our hearts on that which we truly desire and then create a story in our minds to justify the means of attaining it.

This is precisely how generations of Pharaoh "god men" were able to enslave and kill millions of their own people in order to build monuments of pride, all without a hint of guilt. It is the key that has repeatedly opened the door to genocide and religious crusade, to child soldiering and prostitution. It is how those who sit atop the caste system do so without any remorse for those at the bottom, and how certain serial killers, bank robbers and old-west outlaws throughout history have gone to their graves proclaiming their innocence to the bitter end.

In much the same way, I metamorphosed in my mind from being a drug-addicted college student to Savior of the world in just short of three weeks. The process of delusion was set into motion the very moment I began my acid experiment, and while these stories are usually forged over much longer periods of time, in my case, the drugs acted as a major catalyst.

From the very start, I wanted to probe the depths of this new drug and decided to jump in head first, taking ten hits in just the first three days. While I initially found the experience to be quite exhilarating, in the end, acid turned out to be much like every other drug I had ever set my hope on. Over time, the trips became less and less intense, leaving me ultimately unsatisfied and perpetually longing for more.

As a critical component of my quest for the elusive rabbit hole, I had expected this drug to open up an entirely new world for me. Yet beyond the initial feeling of euphoria and some interesting visual effects, my life continued to be quite, well, normal. The drug experience alone had failed to satisfy, and I quickly began searching for something deeper.

One night about a week and a half later while tripping at a friend's house, I locked myself in his spare bedroom and determined not to leave until I discovered the rabbit hole, or the portal from our world to the next. This, I believed, was the key to my Wonderland. I took a seat in the only chair in the room and began to think deeply.

I rationalized that if my consciousness was truly defined by neurological pathways in my brain and nothing more, then my perception of the room, and all of reality for that matter, would likewise be contained completely within the bounds of my own mind. I concluded that through the medium of my thoughts alone, I should be able to manipulate any and all aspects of my perceived reality, thereby creating a new one based on my own desires.

Emboldened by this idea, my mind started racing. *If this is my reality, then I can do anything I want. What then would stop me from creating another person in my mind and having them enter the room at this very instant?* It sounded plausible enough to me, so I decided to give it a shot. I focused my thoughts on the closed door and tried with everything inside of me to make it open. For over an hour, I sat in that chair simply staring at the door and waiting.

I had developed a hunch somewhere along the line that Wonderland was actually a cartoon world, so my honest hope was for someone to visit me from that realm. I tried my hardest to picture Bugs Bunny or Daffy Duck, or better yet one of the ThunderCats, throwing the door wide open and waltzing into my world. We would hang out together all night, playing old board games and swapping stories. Then hopefully they would show me the way to Wonderland.

You can probably guess how that one turned out for me. Once I gave up on this scheme, I started to rack my brain for other masterful plans. *If Wonderland is real, then there must be a way to get there. I just need to find the wormhole to transport me.* I looked around the sparsely furnished room, and finding nothing of interest, I decided that it was time to give up and rejoin my friends. But just as I went to cut off the lights, an idea hit me.

Light travels faster than anything else in the universe. It is both a wave and a particle at the same time, and life is impossible without it. My mind began to search out this profound mystery and finally settled on a thought. *Perhaps light itself is the key that will unlock this secret realm to me.* There was a small desk lamp in the room, so I turned it on and removed the shade, after which I stared directly at the glowing sphere beneath, moving closer and closer until my face was hovering nearly two inches from the bulb.

At first, I convinced myself that the plan was actually working. A dark spot had begun to form in the center of my vision resembling a long tunnel, and I decided that it must be the rabbit hole. I stared at the bulb even more intently than before, hoping and waiting for my breakthrough. And while I don't remember exactly at what point I called it quits, the tunnel never did pan out.

More dazed and confused than ever, I left the room to find my friends.

∞   WONDERLAND   ∞

WHEN I FINALLY CAME TO my senses, I found myself deeply affected by this experience. I had placed such a heavy weight of expectation on this drug that when it did not measure up, my entire world was severely shaken. My hope of finding meaning and purpose in this life had suffered a fatal blow, and for the first time in recent memory, I felt lost. Then to top it off, even my drug buddies stopped hanging out with me because apparently I was acting "strange."

Feeling isolated and alone, I began to think back to my encounter with the supernatural, the day I received the word "peace." Maybe there was more to it than I first realized. Once again, I remembered my convictions from childhood about eternity and discovered a new openness within to the possibility of God's existence. *Maybe there is more to life than what we see on the surface,* I pondered. *More than death. More than rotting in the earth. More than waiting for the sun to burn out.*

Instantly, my mind turned to the theory of time-infinity. I knew that in order for our existence as mortal human beings to prevail against an eternal backdrop—since any finite life span divided by infinity is zero—we would have to be eternal in nature. The existence of infinitely complex matter within an infinitely expanding universe supports this notion, but I still didn't know where to fit eternity into my worldview.

Then it dawned on me. I had been searching for a Wonderland that could be found on the earth during my finite lifespan. *What if it's not here?* I started to ask myself. *What if it exists in a different time and place? What if Wonderland is in fact real, but can only be found on the other side of death?*

This seemed like a real possibility and aligned in many ways with what I had discovered thus far. Time and time again, I had caught glimpses of a world beyond our own—unexplainable colors, transcendent sounds, moments of spiritual incandescence, déjà vu— yet I could never manage to hold on, no matter how hard I tried. I saw the potential for an existence vastly superior to our tumultuous lives here on earth and envisioned a new world of unparalleled beauty and peace.

For this to happen, though, I knew that a major transformation would have to occur. I could see even then that human beings are, more often than not, the very source of the problems we face here on earth. If there is a better world out there, we certainly do not belong in it. Not in our present state, at least. No, for Wonderland to exist, something would have to give—and that something was us.

While it had been years since I had last thought about my Christian upbringing, I recalled a principle from the faith that fit with these observations. The Bible says that human beings are inherently flawed and that our poor behavior is a direct manifestation of the imperfect nature that exists inside each one of us. Violence, war and human atrocities of every kind are all the consequences of our faulty nature.

As I began to sort through the implications of such an idea, still another Christian concept came to mind, one that I couldn't believe I had overlooked until now. The entire Christian faith is founded on the conviction that God designed mankind to live forever with him in paradise, the place we commonly refer to as heaven. *How could I have missed this?* I implored. *Christians believe in Wonderland!*

I had never before made the connection between Wonderland and heaven because for so long, I had refused to engage along the lines of the eternal. But now that I was once again open to that possibility, I could clearly see the parallel. As I remembered it, Christians believe heaven to be a new world that lies on the other side of death, a place without any strife or conflict whatsoever. Human beings will live there with God and with one another in a state of perfect peace and total bliss for all of eternity.

But how could this be? I thought. *How could crazy humans, who can't get along here on earth, suddenly start living in peace just because they die and get carried off to a different place? If we remain the same as we are now, the next world is going to have the same exact problems that this one has.* I pondered this dilemma for quite some time before the solution came to me. It was strikingly simple—the ultimate Sunday school response—yet somehow I had been unable to see it until now. The answer was Jesus.

According to the Bible, Jesus Christ is the only person on the planet who ever lived a completely perfect life. He allegedly never cheated on a test, lied to his mom or stole anything. What's more, he never so much as harbored a single impure or hateful thought. He loved all of mankind without exception and lived his life from birth to death as a perfect channel of God's love.

Before Jesus, according to the story, there was a barrier that stood between human beings and the God who created us. Although every person on earth was designed to live in close relationship with God, no one was able to do so because no one was able to live up to his perfect standard. While some were able to achieve better records than others, everyone inevitably fell short in the end, and the great divide between God and humanity remained.

Christians believe that this is the very reason why Jesus came to earth, to bridge that gap. The story goes that Jesus lived flawlessly, thereby meeting God's righteous standard. He was then executed on a cross to pay the penalty for the wrong-doing of the entire human race. It continues that three days after his death, Jesus rose from the grave to propose an exchange, offering to give his perfect record to all who believe in him and thereby creating a way for mankind to live in unbroken relationship with God.

Jesus' resurrection is the bedrock of the Christian faith because it provides a solution to mankind's most impossible problem—death. The idea is that if he could come back from the grave himself, then he would be able to bring others back as well. This, according to the story, is why Jesus hung around on the earth so long after his resurrection, to demonstrate his power over death.

The Bible says that after forty full days, Jesus returned to heaven under the premise that he would come back to the earth at the end of time to judge every human being who has ever lived. After that final judgment, the story concludes with the destruction of the earth and the establishment of God's eternal kingdom, the Wonderland I had been searching for. At that time, all who have received Jesus' perfect righteousness will be allowed to enter and will live there in peace forever.

What a story! I thought. *This is great!* Not only had God revealed himself to me, now it looked like I would find my Wonderland after all. Before this revelation, I had come to terms with the fact that I was part of the human quagmire; that is, stuck to a giant rock floating through space and awaiting my inevitable death. Other than a handful of astronauts, this is pretty much the sad reality of the entire human race.

With that morbid notion bouncing around in my mind, it only made sense that I would be drawn to the person of Jesus. As far as I could tell, he was the only chance of me getting out of this predicament alive. I had no choice about whether I would die or not. That much had already been settled. Now it seemed that I had a new option—to be raised up. And I was all for it.

If death was my quagmire, Jesus Christ was my exit strategy.

∞ A ROMANCE NOVEL SUICIDE ∞

WHILE INITIALLY THE STORY of Jesus brought a ray of hope back into my world, I soon found myself feeling dissatisfied once again. For years, I had envisioned the moment when I would discover Wonderland and share my breakthrough with the world, rising instantly to success and emerging ultimately as one of the most influential people in history.

By contrast, this Jesus stuff seemed way too simple. *Was I supposed to just get in line and march along with all of the other humdrum Christians? Did God really want me to become another boring churchgoer? Why would God have revealed all of this to me unless he wanted me to do something about it? If I were meant to be a mere spectator, why show me anything at all?*

Fixated on the moment when God had personally visited me and sent me the message of peace, I began to reconsider the story. I had perceived from the get-go that it was my role to pave the way for others, yet now it appeared that Jesus had already done all of the heavy lifting. *Was there anything left for me to accomplish?* As I mulled over the possibilities, I realized that there was still one very important role left to play. Jesus had already come and gone—the first time. But according to the story, his return is imminent. *Could I possibly be the Second Coming?*

I started gathering evidence in my mind and immediately saw alignment all around. First, I considered my name, Matthew, which just so happens to be the first book of the New Testament. It also contains two T's, or crosses, symbolizing the Second Messiah. My hometown of Charleston is known as the Holy City and has the exact same latitude as Israel, where Jesus lived. Plus, I was living almost precisely two thousand years after his first coming. *These signs can only point to one thing—I must be the Savior.*

Practically overnight, I made the seamless transition from college student to Second Coming, rewriting my entire life story to incorporate an unparalleled level of ultimate purpose and eternal significance. It only made sense to me that I should play a central role in the unfolding epic of our universe, to be the protagonist of not just a worldly drama, but a cosmic one. Thus, I assumed the very role of God himself.

Yet somehow during the process of building this story in my mind, I never once considered the years of drinking, drugging, lying, cheating, stealing, gambling and sleeping around that had defined the last season of my life. I didn't even think for a moment that perhaps God incarnate would take it upon himself to live up to a slightly higher standard than that.

In fact, I held firmly to my conviction that the moral framework imposed upon society through organized religion was precisely what had held people down for so long. I believed that it was by breaking away from meaningless rules and empty ritual that I had finally been able to reach the level of personal freedom necessary to fulfill my destiny. Like an Ayn Rand protagonist, I had become the quintessential man.

Suddenly, I understood why God had waited so long to reveal himself to me. As with Jesus so many years before, God needed to prepare me before he could inform me of my true identity, in order that I would be fully equipped when the time came to carry out his master plan. Now that I had been primed, God was going to use me to finish the process of redemption that he had begun on the cross of

Jesus Christ. The foundation had been laid, and I was going to bring it to completion.

Blinded by sheer pride, I slipped deeper and deeper into my delusional state with no ability to see the host of warning signs that should have stopped me dead in my tracks. Although some were more painfully obvious than others, there was one in particular that had I recognized at the time, could have easily deterred me from carrying on. It comes from a story in the Bible that is set mere moments after Jesus' ascension into heaven, forty days after his resurrection from the dead.

As could be expected after watching a man float off into space, the assembled crowd continued to stare blankly into the now empty sky, mouths agape. With their eyes still fixed on the point where Jesus had disappeared from sight, two men in white robes approached and addressed the group. "Men of Galilee," they begin in the first chapter of the book of Acts, "why do you stand looking into heaven? This Jesus, who was taken up from you into heaven, will come in the same way as you saw him go into heaven."

As it turns out, while I got the part right about Jesus returning to the earth, I totally missed the memo about how he would do it. He came into our world the first time as a human being born of a human mother. But the second time, according to the story, he will come out of the sky in unmistakable fashion. I must have missed the day we covered that in Sunday school.

Yet rather than consulting the Bible even once to investigate my claims, the story evolved in my mind unchecked. As the self-proclaimed Messiah, I embraced an elevated sense of importance that lifted me high above other normal people. In fact, I was so steeped in arrogance that I didn't even think to pray one single time during the entire ordeal.

In the end, though, I do not believe my story arose so much out of denial as it did from pure delusion. LSD is a powerful drug, and it continued to have a strong effect on my mind even between my active trips. The story became such a part of me that it consumed all sense of my reality, and I completely lost the ability to decipher what was real and what was not.

While I had always prided myself in keeping my secret life hidden behind a façade, the two had finally become indistinguishable in my mind. When I first started living as a doppelganger, I thought for sure that I would never cease to be able to fool my parents, my friends and everyone else for that matter. Yet all of a sudden, the only person I was fooling was myself.

As my wheels continued to spin at breakneck speed, the story progressed further. I began to think about how my predecessor Jesus had had to die in order to fulfill his purpose and concluded that I would most likely need to do the same. The difference being that upon my death, the day of final judgment would be ushered in, and the world as we know it would cease to exist. I was the very last piece of the cosmic puzzle, the only thing left standing in the way of God's eternal kingdom.

As I wondered how God would have me die, a curious thought seemed to prevail in my mind. It came from a rather unlikely source, a 19th century romance novel from my middle school reading list entitled *The Awakening* by Kate Chopin. In the story, the protagonist becomes worn down after a life fraught with difficulty and disappointment, ultimately deciding to kill herself in the ocean.

The book concludes with a description of this woman swimming out past the surf, away from all of the problems and despair of this world, where she slips painlessly under the water—a noble escape from this chaotic life into the quiet nothingness of death.

In full romantic fashion, the scene wholly neglects the gruesome reality of death and somehow makes drowning in the ocean sound like a peaceful way to die. And considering how utterly delusional I was, it's not surprising that I bought into this description so unreservedly. I assumed that I would just swim out into the great blue yonder and pass right on through from this world into the next.

After wrestling with this idea for quite some time, it was the complete randomness of the thought which led me to the conclusion that it had come from above. Drowning certainly wouldn't have been my first preference, but I realized that the manner of my death paled in comparison to what was truly at stake—my triumphant return to God's heavenly kingdom and the unimaginable glory that awaited me there.

Yet when the moment to die arrived, and I forced my body under the surface of the swaying sea, I discovered a very different place than I had expected. There was nothing glorious or romantic about what I found there, no fanfare or angels holding up banners with my name on it. Instead, it was dark and cold and, well, utterly horrible. As I pushed my body down deeper, I could feel my lungs contracting and the pressure building more and more. I stayed under until I could stand it no longer, then almost as an unconscious reflex, my body shot to the surface.

A wave of fear, panic and doubt raced through my mind, followed by an aftershock of what I can only describe as debilitating terror. *Is this really what I signed up for? Is it truly my time to die?* I plunged again and again beneath the water's surface, trying with all of my might to keep my body under. I desperately wanted to embrace the nothingness and let go—of life and breath—of everything.

But with each consecutive attempt, the life force deep within the core of my being fought back. I would hold my body down as long as humanly possible, and then before I knew it, I would manage to struggle back to the surface. Again and again, I plunged. Again and again, I rose. It was like an automatic override that I couldn't bypass. I simply could not stop breathing.

Frustrated and tired, I finally rose to the surface to regroup. I had reached the thin film that separates this world from the next, the threshold known on this side as death. Yet the closer got, the less I recognized it. Like all of the hollow men before me, I found that my world was about to end, not with a bang, but with a whimper. And as I stared death squarely in the face, I realized that it wasn't anything like I imagined it would be.

Rather than peaceful quiet, there was eerie silence. Rather than a world of comforting light, I found a place of suffocating darkness.

CHAPTER FOUR

THE SANCTUARY

"C—c—c—CAN I HAVE a t—t—t—towel?" I asked the two couples soaking in the hot tub. I had spotted a boardwalk down the beach a ways from where I landed and had found my way up to a spacious pool deck. A few seconds passed, yet the blank stares did not change. I began to wonder if they had heard me. Granted my articulation couldn't have been stellar, but considering the circumstances, I felt that I had communicated fairly well. *Perhaps they're offended,* I thought. *I am covering myself the best I can.*

Since I didn't have a whole lot of other recourse, I decided that they would just have to deal. Sure, they were on vacation at a five star resort. And sure, a large naked person who had wandered in off the beach was interrupting their precious hot tub time. But sometimes you've just got to help a dude out.

A few more seconds passed with no response, and right as I was beginning to consider plan B, I noticed a hand slowly emerging from the steamy water. With pointer finger extended, it indicated a group of chairs no more than ten yards away, where a stack of towels sat neatly folded. This first sign of life had been initiated by one of the guys, who finally broke the hanging silence. "Yeah man," he said hesitantly. "There are some, uh, towels over there."

The man's face returned to its original vacant stare, and with hand still raised, the entire scene remained motionless as if frozen in time. Since our interaction had already carried me over the recommended daily value of awkward, I nodded to express my gratitude and took off in the direction of the chairs. I reached the stack of towels and quickly grabbed one before collapsing on a chaise lounge. *Whew!* I thought to myself as I covered my exposed body. *Glad that's over.*

I must not have made a big impression on the folks in the jacuzzi because I never heard from them again. I was so relieved to be back on solid ground that at the time, I didn't think twice about the fact that they never came over to check on me. And why should they? For all they knew, I was just some college kid who had gone out for a late night skinny dip in the ocean.

There was no way for them to know that I wasn't a guest of the Sanctuary Hotel or that I had never even set foot inside the building. I gave them no indication that I was totally lost or that I didn't have a clue what beach I had just walked up from. And although my lungs ached and I desperately needed medical attention, it would have been impossible for them to know that from the outside.

I mean, who in their right mind would have guessed that the-six-foot six, 225 pound naked man asking for a towel at 11:30 p.m. on the deck of a Kiawah Island beach resort could possibly have started swimming at 5:30 a.m. that morning in front of Folly Beach?

No, I could never blame them for not acting, mainly because I know with absolute certainty that I would have done the same exact thing had I been put in their position. I know this because I strongly believe in self-preservation and because I happen to have a protocol for what to do when confronted by a naked person in public. Hold still, back away slowly and if that doesn't work, curl up into a ball. It's easy to remember because it is the same thing I do when I see a bear. I stay out of a lot of trouble that way.

Fortunately for me, though, there was another couple on the deck that night. They had been swimming in the lap pool and came over to check on me not long after my arrival. I imagine that once they had watched me lie still as a corpse for a minute or two, curiosity must have gotten the better of them. They approached tentatively, interested to see if I was alright.

Rather than trying to explain what had happened, I decided to simply ask them to call for help. They immediately looked at one another, pausing briefly as if for a moment of silent negotiation, and then both hustled off in the direction of the hotel. I guess neither wanted the job of staying behind to keep the naked guy company. Regardless, I was glad to be alone again with my thoughts, this time relieved to know that help was on its way.

∞ WHAT WOULD JESUS DO ∞

FROM THE VERY MOMENT I got my hands on the LSD, it was the beginning of the end for me. I took two hits the first night and eight the second; after that, things get a bit hazy. I do know that I spent a week at my friend's house and that I flew directly back to Charleston from there. Aside from that, the only other detail I remember is a burning desire to see my hometown through the lens of this new drug I had found.

I didn't wait long after landing in Charleston to begin my next trip, taking four hits of LSD on the shuttle from the Charleston International Airport to my house on the Battery downtown. If you've never seen LSD, you might be surprised by the fact that the thirty hits I purchased consisted of one square sheet of decorated paper about the size of my two thumbs put together.

The drug is produced in liquid form and applied to what is known as blotting paper, which absorbs the drug solution and is then divided into hits approximately one quarter of a square inch in size. Don't let the size fool you—each tiny square packs a big punch. The fifteen or so hits that I had remaining turned out to be enough to send me off the deep end.

I had stashed the drugs in a CD case buried deep inside my carry-on, and as soon as I got on the shuttle, I carefully separated the four hits and placed them squarely on my tongue. There were several other passengers taking the shuttle that night who had to be dropped off before me, and my house was the very last stop. By the time we got there, I was so high that I could barely figure out how to pay the driver.

Fortunately, my parents were out of town at the time, so I dropped off my bags and embarked upon the first of several epic acid journeys through the streets of downtown Charleston. I walked from my house at the very tip of the peninsula, weaving my way through the familiar, often one-way streets to upper King, where swarms of college students would line the sidewalks each night as they moved from bar to bar.

Although these epic nights do blend together in my memory, there is one in particular that stands out among all of the others. It was my last trip before the swim, and my Messiah story had already taken deep root in my mind. I had eight hits of acid left in total, so I took four and walked from my house to a bar on Market Street where I had planned to meet a couple of friends to watch a local band. The music was good, but my friends were a bit weirded out by the drugs and left soon after I got there.

I hung out at the bar for a while longer and eventually decided it was time to get some fresh air. I walked across the street and sat down on a table in the pavilion where merchants sell sweetgrass baskets and stone-ground grits to well-meaning folks all the way from Ohio. As I sat reflecting on the scene before me, an older black man carrying a tall boy in a paper bag approached me asking for money.

Seeing as how part of my job as Messiah was to bring good news to the poor, I gave him some cash and struck up a conversation with him. He told me how he had been down on his luck and how he had not been able to work due to an injured hand. Unable to make ends meet, he had been forced to live on the street. I listened with a compassionate ear and truly desired to help the man.

After a few moments, an idea popped into my head. "I can heal your hand," I said confidently. The man shot his glance at me and began to search out my unflinching face, squinting with wrinkled brow as if trying to recognize an old friend. He obviously did not believe in my ability to carry through on my promise because ultimately he just shrugged and took a swig of his beer.

Despite my new friend's lack of faith, I remained convinced of my ability to heal and addressed him once again. "Let me see your hand," I implored. The man looked over at me again, only this time with eyes wide open. *This guy's not kidding*, they spoke silently. He glanced at me and then down at the ground, and after finally resting his gaze upon my stern face, he slowly extended his right hand.

"This one," he said. As I clasped his hand in mine, I could see the man visibly wince in pain. At least I knew the injury was real. I placed my other hand on the outside of his and began to slowly guide our hands through a series of different positions, as if we were performing some elaborate handshake that we had practiced hundreds of times before.

Occasionally, I could detect discomfort on his face when I moved too quickly, but for the most part, he just continued to stare wide-eyed at our interlocked hands, mesmerized by the spectacle unfolding before him. I must have genuinely gotten his hopes up because when I finally let go of his hand, he went to test it out. Immediately, he recoiled in pain. After a few moments, I couldn't stand it any longer and asked him if his hand had in fact been miraculously healed. "It feels...better," he said shakily.

Perhaps it was the alcohol talking or the 40 dollars I had given him minutes earlier or both. Maybe he had admired my zeal and simply didn't want to let me down. Either way, it was clear as day that this man had no more been healed than I had walked on water. Yet rather than listening to his physical cues, I latched onto his thin response and made up my mind that I had done something really special.

Since my friends had already left, I no longer had anything to do and decided to ask the man if there was any way I could help him. He had mentioned before that he was hungry and brought it up again, so I began thinking of restaurants that would still be open. A popular late night pizza place around the corner on King Street immediately came to mind, and we started off in that direction, continuing our conversation on the way.

As we walked, we encountered several other destitute men and women who were out begging for cash. Normally, I would have had no problem averting my eyes and continuing down the sidewalk, but not this night. *I mean, what would Jesus do?* He certainly wouldn't turn a deaf ear to those in his path asking for help, particularly since I had more than enough money to feed them all. So despite the adamant protest of my companion, I invited them to come along.

As we walked, my original friend continued to insist that we leave the others behind. He told me how dangerous they were and how he was the only one I could trust. He explained that they were only out to get my money and that he was my only true friend. At the time, I couldn't understand why this man was so resistant to helping others. But when I discovered the next day that I had given away more than two hundred dollars over the course of the night, I realized that he probably just saw me as a walking ATM machine and wanted to withdraw as much as he could.

Since he wasn't the only one who caught on to this, a small posse began to form around us as we walked down Market Street. His futile attempt to dissuade the others caused quite a racket, and despite my tireless efforts to make peace, the bickering continued.

As the walk was rather lengthy, a few in the group turned back at various points along the way. When we arrived at the pizza shop, I was escorted by two homeless men and one woman. There was some dispute over where to eat—one wanted Chinese and another wanted Mexican—but I reassured them that this was the only restaurant open within five or six blocks. Tired from walking, we ended the debate and entered the restaurant.

After a noisy discussion with the girl behind the counter, we settled on chicken wings over pizza and ordered two dozen so that each of us could choose a flavor. We all got drinks, and following a second raucous scene at the soda fountain, we sat in a booth to wait for our order. I used the opportunity to continue teaching my new friends out of my infinite wisdom and informed them about how God wanted all of us to exist peacefully and how he would surely provide for their needs.

The food finally arrived, and just as we were beginning to eat, a friend from high school walked in. He instantly recognized me and came over to our table looking quite perplexed. I offered him some chicken wings and told him that he was welcome to join us, but he didn't appear interested.

He asked me what I was up to, so I informed him that my friends and I were enjoying a late dinner. We talked for a moment more, but he just kept laughing to himself and looking around the restaurant as if he expected the crew of Candid Camera to pop out at any moment. *He had no way to understand*, I thought. *These are my sheep, and I am simply doing what any good shepherd would do— feeding them.*

Once everyone had finished eating, I invited the group to walk back to the market with me. But the woman informed us that she was headed north, which was enough to sway one of the guys to go the same way. I gave them both twenty dollars and bid them farewell. Once again, it was down to only me and my very first comrade, the one with the injured hand, and he was livid. He could not imagine why I had given all of that money away to those no-good, worthless street people.

I tried to reason with him, but he did not want to hear anything I had to say. The last straw came when I gave away some money in passing to a man who had abandoned our group earlier. Outraged, my companion waited for us to turn a corner, looked to see that we were out of sight and then leapt to attack me.

Considering that the man was unarmed and that I outweighed him by at least fifty pounds, his assault was unsuccessful. I simply grabbed both of his forearms and held him off until he gave up. Once I let go of his arms, he paused for a moment and tried his maneuver again with the same result. While I had not been hurt, it was clearly time to part ways. I had tried with all of my power to help this man, and he had fought me every step of the way. I thought about Jesus and remembered how he had likewise been rejected.

After leaving the man, I headed back to the Battery and began to reflect upon my night. I remembered all of the people I had helped and how grateful they had been. All but one had received me with thankfulness, and in that case, I had even faced persecution for my generosity.

Jesus was persecuted for helping people. Why shouldn't I expect the same? No one said this would be an easy road. It may be difficult now, but what's a little pain in light of eternity?

∞ OBEY ∞

As I WALKED, I pulled my iPod out of my pocket and began shuffling through my favorite playlist. Every song that came on seemed to be addressed directly to me, as if they were personal serenades from God himself. The full moon bathed the streets in blue light, and I danced down East Bay Street past Rainbow Row and finally over to the High Battery. "Mysterious Ways" by U2 started playing, and I listened intently to the lyrics of the first verse:

> Johnny, take a walk / With your sister the moon / Let her pale light in / To fill up your room / You've been living underground / Eating from a can / You've been running away / From what you don't understand.

As the words washed over me, I knew what I had to do. Just as my brother, Jesus, had done, I also had to go the way of the cross. I thought about the moment when he first found out the frightening news that he would be brutally executed. *What went through his mind?* The song continued to play, and as I listened to the second verse, my conviction only grew deeper:

> Johnny, take a dive / With your sister in the rain / Let her talk about the things / You can't explain / To touch is to heal / To hurt is to steal / If you want to kiss the sky / Better learn how to kneel / On your knees boy.

Electricity pulsed through my veins. I imagined the glory that would be manifested when I left my mortal body and "kissed the sky" through my death. Yet at the same time, I felt the fear gripping me tightly, repeatedly bringing me back to this call to die. I oscillated back and forth between excitement and pure dread as the tears streamed down my face.

In overly dramatic fashion, I began to stagger down the street, feeling "stricken" as I agonized over my fate. I finally picked my head up and found myself two feet away from a stop sign. I looked more closely and noticed a familiar sticker on the bottom right-hand corner of the sign bearing the image of Andre the Giant, a famous pro wrestler from the 1980s. It read simply, "Obey."

A sign from God! I suddenly felt strengthened as all of my remaining doubt evaporated into thin air. I climbed up the steps to the High Battery, and peering down the length of it, I saw a vision of a boardwalk extending from the Battery wall out over the Charleston Harbor. Tears immediately started forming in my eyes, and at that moment, I knew how I was to die. Jesus had been lifted up on the cross—I would sink down into the ocean.

Since drowning had always been a major fear of mine, the thought alone was enough to make my blood run cold. A movie came to mind entitled *The Perfect Storm* about a ship that went down in an ocean squall with several crew members still aboard. The scene depicted the men watching helplessly as the water rose around them until there was no air left in the cabin. They each took one final breath and simply waited for the life to be choked out of them by the cruel ocean water.

Despite this painful image, I remained convinced that this was my call and tried to embrace my fate. With tears still running down my face, I took a seat with my back against the Battery wall and put my head in my hands. When I finally looked up, a man was standing over me and peering down to see if I was alright. He quickly noticed my tears and took a seat next to me before introducing himself.

I don't remember his name or anything about the man other than the fact that he was coming down from a meth trip and that he was going to talk to Mayor Joe Riley about planting Bermuda grass, which apparently has incredible shade resistance, at White Point Gardens. We watched the sunrise together and chatted about nothing, but as I have never been a fan of small talk, my attention was waning fast. Then out of the blue, he said something that perked my ears.

Without any prompting, he proceeded to tell me how one of his favorite things to do in the whole world was to swim naked in the ocean at Folly Beach County Park. Although I had never even been there prior to our conversation, the idea instantly stuck in my mind. I had only learned minutes before that it was my destiny to die in the water, and here God was already giving me the next piece of the puzzle.

As I walked home that morning alongside droves of early morning joggers, my mind was churning in high gear. Since I could not figure out why someone would offer up such information to a complete stranger, I took it to be yet another sign. I now knew how my life would end—and where I would fulfill my eternal destiny.

∞   I AM MATTHEW   ∞

"WAKE UP, HONEY...Wake up. It is twelve fifteen, and you have officially slept through the entire morning." I opened my eyes, and sure enough, there was my mom hovering over me like a mother hen. Still in bed after my long night on LSD, I knew she had come in to jump start my day. Although she was pretty good about letting me sleep, as soon as afternoon rolled around, all bets were off.

Since I was still a bit starry eyed from the night before, it took me longer than normal to respond. She noticed that I was acting strange and asked me if everything was alright. I paused for a few moments and contemplated what an appropriate answer might be for this particular situation. Since the Messiah did happen to be living under her roof, I decided it would be courteous to at least inform her.

I paused for just a moment more, looked her straight in the eyes and said in my gentlest Messiah voice, "Mom, I'm Matthew." Her face immediately went blank, and she began to stare at me like I was from outer space. Although she didn't say anything, I can only imagine what she was thinking. *Really? What a shocker. That's only what I named you 21 years ago.*

Since she obviously did not get the picture, I proceeded to elaborate upon my statement. "Mom, I am Matthew…Matt–hew," I continued in almost a whisper. "The Second Coming of Jesus."

Her jaw dropped. I could see the alarms going off in her head as her mom-radar escalated straight to code red. Her face was pensive, as if she were searching for the right words to say, yet she remained silent.

While I didn't have a great read on her, I could tell that she wasn't receiving the news so well and tried to console her. "It's ok, Mom, this is a good thing. God sent me here and…"

She must have already heard enough because she cut me off midsentence. "Are you on drugs?" she snapped.

I didn't miss a beat. "Yeah," I said casually. "But just LSD."

Her face was once again expressionless. All of those years spent cradling me as a baby, chasing after me as a toddler, disciplining me as a young child, bearing with me as a teenager and directing me as a 21-year-old suddenly came to a head. I'm surprised she didn't fall over. Instead, she very gently sat down on the edge of my bed and looked off into the corner of the room. I think she was trying to decide whether to be upset with me, sad for herself or simply terrified that her very own son had lost his mind.

I desperately wanted to explain to her how God had revealed himself to me and chosen me to be his messenger of peace. I longed to tell her the significance of my name and how all of the signs clearly pointed to my identity as the Second Coming. I wanted to paint a picture of the glory that awaited me on the other side of death and how I would happily share it with her and with our whole family. But ultimately I knew that she would need time to process, so I remained silent.

Finally, she gathered herself and with tears in her eyes, began to speak. She told me about how she had tried various drugs in the '70s and how they had never led to anything good. She warned me about the dangers of taking such a strong drug as LSD and explained how it alters one's sense of reality. Then she sternly forbid me from using any more drugs and made me promise that I would stop cold turkey.

I could tell that she was barely holding herself together, so I quickly consented and tried to comfort her with an embrace. She stayed long enough to shed a few tears on my shoulder and then left the room to find my father. After a brief discussion, they decided that I was to be under house arrest until further notice. Petrified I might do something foolish, I found out later that they nearly had me committed.

Rather than put up a fight, I decided it would be best just to go with the flow. My parents weren't able to see how wonderful this news truly was; and not just for me, but for them as well. It isn't every day you find out that your son is the Messiah. In my mind, they should have been rejoicing with me, yet I knew they had concerns about the drugs. They did not understand how LSD had opened my eyes and set me free. Clearly their minds were still very much closed.

I decided that the best way to enlighten them would be to spend some quality time together. Maybe this house arrest would even work in my favor, providing them with a chance to get to know the new and improved me. Then they would clearly see the finger of God at work in my life and accept the inevitable—that I truly was the Messiah of the world.

While I knew that I wouldn't be able to share the details of my impending death, I wanted them to at least understand what was going on when the world suddenly came to an end.

∞   MOMENT OF TRUTH   ∞

AFTER A FEW DAYS, the tension in the house had died down, and I was eager to get on with my plan. Unfortunately my parents hadn't come around like I had expected, so I started thinking of a way to get them off my back. I had hidden plenty of things from them in the past and didn't see why this should be any different. I would just make something up.

As I pondered the question of what to tell them, I had a moment of clarity and started writing what turned into a full-on speech. After several practice runs alone in my room, I approached my parents. "Mom, Dad," I began with feigned remorse. "I am really sorry. I'm sorry that I let drugs become so important to me. I'm sorry that I told you I was Jesus. But most of all, I'm sorry that I hurt you. I know that what I did was wrong, and I've seen the light. I realize how damaging drugs truly can be, and I want you to know that I'm done with them for good."

On and on I went, ending with a sincere promise to attend church with them in the morning. When I finally delivered the address to my parents in the living room, I felt like an actor on stage. Everything was planned, from my inflection and pauses to my hand gestures and strategic knee bends. The entire production was so coated with artificial sincerity that I'm surprised they bought it.

Yet they did. I think deep down they really wanted to believe that I meant what I said. And to their credit, they weren't nearly as convinced as I thought they were. I was under the impression that my dazzling performance had wowed the audience and that I would be off the hook for good. Unbeknownst to me, they were still very much considering the psych ward.

Immediately following my speech, I left the house and drove straight to a friend's apartment on James Island with my last four hits of acid. I had promised him two, and as hard as it was for me to part with them, I wanted to stay true to my word. We both took two hits around 8 p.m. on the night of May 28, 2005 and began our trip. As soon as the acid hit my tongue, I returned full tilt to Second Coming mode. Although I had bought some candy and soda for the night, I never so much as touched it. I was not about to be distracted by anything and remained focused on the task at hand.

All night long, I oscillated between feelings of excitement and dread as I started to think through the reality of my upcoming ordeal. I searched myself for the courage to face my fear and the strength to overcome this final hurdle. Several hours into the trip, I decided that I would watch some TV to calm my nerves. *The Big Lebowski* was on, and I quickly came to the conclusion that the entire movie had been designed by God for this very moment in time, a deduction primarily based on a psychedelic scene where a bowling alley shoe rack forms a stairway to heaven. I knew this was a sign just for me.

My friend came in and tried to get me to lighten up a couple of times, but my unwavering intensity ultimately deterred him, and he spent the rest of the night off doing his own thing. Once the movie ended, I knew that I was as ready as I would ever be. I hung around the house for another couple of minutes, climbed into the silver Audi A4 that was my car at the time and took off toward the beach.

I could barely see the road through my tears as I drove to Folly Beach and stayed well under the speed limit. There were almost no cars out, and once I got to Folly, I slowed down to a crawl. I wiped my face with my hand as I looked for my turn, and sure enough, right where the man said it would be, there was the sign for Folly Beach County Park. With racing pulse, I hung a right and began the last leg of my drive.

I reached the park at 5 a.m. and found the front gate closed. I pulled up as far as I could to read the hours of operation and realized that the park didn't open until later in the morning. I thought about moving my car, but since I had no intention of coming back, I just left it blocking the entrance. The way I saw it, the whole world was going to end in a matter of hours, so what difference would it make if the County Park was open or not.

I grabbed my iPod and cigarettes out of the car and started walking toward the beach. The salt air and crashing waves overwhelmed my senses, releasing a surge of adrenaline that ran through my entire body. Tears once again flooded my eyes. The scene was beginning to feel all too real, and I pictured Jesus in the Garden of Gethsemane. Just like him, I too was stricken—a Man of Sorrows—about to sacrifice myself for the sake of the world.

The moment I arrived at the beach and caught sight of the water, doubt flooded my mind. *Am I really about to go through with this? Do I have the will to actually end my own life?* While I knew what had to be done, I suddenly found myself crippled by fear. I needed something to push me over the edge, but I didn't know what. As I took off my shirt to help me get prepared, my sense of dread only grew stronger. *Am I ready to die?*

With tears continuing to flow, I paced the beach tirelessly. Back and forth I walked. Back and forth my mind fluxed. *Go or stay. Life or death. Safety or glory.* At wits end, I begged the heavens for a sign. I would go willingly, yet I needed something, one final confirmation that this truly was my destiny.

I waited and waited, and just as I was about to give up the hope of receiving a supernatural go-ahead, I noticed a small movement in the distance. I watched intently as two Folly Beach police officers came into my line of sight, walking directly toward where I stood on the beach. As they approached, I froze like a deer in headlights. *What are they doing here?* I wondered. *Could this be my sign?*

Although they were still a long way off, I realized that if I could see them, they could see me. I had no idea what to do, so I stood motionless and simply waited. I don't know if the sand slowed them down or if they were just taking their sweet time, but it felt like an eternity before they finally reached me. All I could hear the whole time was the sound of my heart pounding inside of my chest.

"Hey, Buddy," the first officer called out. "What's going on here?"

I tried to think of how to answer such an open ended question, but my mind drew a complete blank. Since I didn't want to say the wrong thing, I simply remained silent. The only thing I could think about was whether or not I would be able to outrun them to the water. They waited for a reply, and when they realized that I wasn't going to speak, the second officer broke the silence.

"This here is a private beach," he began, "which means that you're trespassing. Do you realize that?"

Again, I searched my mind for an appropriate response, but the fear lay like a shroud over my thoughts, and ultimately I found none. Consumed with ideas of escape, my attention remained fixed on one thing—getting to the water. I *had* to get to the water. Several seconds went by before the first officer spoke again.

"Are you on drugs or something?" he asked. "You're standing there like a tin soldier."

A tin soldier. Instantly, my mind raced back to that fateful night in my apartment, the night God gave me the word "peace," my very first sign. *This is it. This is the confirmation I asked for. There's no turning back now.*

"No, officer," I managed to utter as I reached into my pockets. "Just startled, that's all." I proceeded to pull out my keys, my iPod and my cigarettes, holding them out like an offering in my hands. The first cop stepped forward to take a closer look and at the same time asked for identification, so I handed him my wallet as well. The second officer then instructed me to hold out my arms and quickly patted me down.

After closely inspecting my cigarettes one by one, the first officer opened up my wallet and removed my driver's license. He studied it for a moment and seemingly satisfied with his search, handed my effects back to me. I could hardly believe my eyes. It appeared that I was off the hook.

Yet no sooner than I had put my things away, the first officer spoke up one final time. "You'll need to come with us."

Wait a minute, I thought. *I'm totally clean. They have no grounds to arrest me.* I racked my brain and after a moment, remembered what they had said about the beach being private. I was trespassing, and now they were going to take me in for it. I knew that this was my moment of truth, the split second where heroes are made—and where cowards are too. So I took off running toward the ocean.

To be honest, I'm not sure if they chased me or not because I never looked back. My guess is that they ran after me down to the water, but what police officer is going to jump in the ocean with all of his gear on to go after a kid on a trespassing charge?

Upon reaching the water, I high-stepped through the surf until I was nearly waist deep and then dove in head first. The police officers must have alerted the Coast Guard right away because the boat I saw passed by no more than ten minutes later. All day long, I thought about how daring my escape had been, but as I learned later, the cops were never going to arrest me.

Turns out they just wanted me to move my car.

∞   A HEAVENLY CHORUS   ∞

FINALLY IN THE WATER, I swam harder than I ever had before. Deep down, I knew no one was behind me, but I wasn't about to take any chances. I wanted to get as far away from that beach as possible. The incident with the cops scared me, not because I was so afraid of being arrested. No, a trespassing charge I could handle. What truly frightened me was the thought of facing my parents.

As I mentioned earlier, my mother and father were one step away from committing me *before* I lied to them, took drugs and proceeded to run from the police into the ocean. I couldn't imagine that whole incident going over too well with them. In fact, I knew exactly what was waiting for me at home—a nice long stay at the insane asylum. I had yanked their chain one too many times, and there was only one course of action left for them to take. And to be honest, I'm just not that into padded walls.

More importantly to me, though, I really did believe my story. I had received the confirmation I asked for, and my confidence had been wholly restored. I was far too invested to back out now. I spent all morning swimming out to sea as I rejoiced over the beauty of the water. I watched the sunrise and imagined the triumphant procession of angels that would be waiting for me when I finally reached the pearly gates.

I felt the warmth of the sun beating down on my face and saw God's angels all around me. In my mind's eye, I pictured a familiar drawing by one of my favorite artists, M.C. Escher, who is famous for his pristine tessellations. In this particular piece, a multitude of beautiful angels fit perfectly together with one another, and I could see them in the sky shining their unyielding approval down upon me.

"Go, Matthew, go," they seemed to say. "You're almost there!"

I imagined the celebration that awaited me in heaven, envisioning the crowd hoisting me up on their shoulders and carrying me into the Holy City. I heard the voice of God commending me for my valiant sacrifice and proclaiming my victory to all of heaven. I basked in the warm and comforting touch of grace as it surrounded me, and I knew that I was finally going home. The world was coming to a close, and I was at the center of the action.

Yet in the midst of my daydreaming, I remained dead set on the task at hand. I knew that there would be plenty of time to rejoice later and made sure to keep one thing and one thing only in the forefront of my mind—getting the job done. *Just a little longer, Matthew,* I told myself again and again. *Just a little longer.*

After hours and hours of swimming, I reached the point where I could no longer see land in any direction and determined that it was time to die. Out of patience and ready for my heavenly reception, I decided to bring the chapter to a close—so I plunged my body into the deep.

CHAPTER FIVE

TO TELL THE TRUTH

THE SANCTUARY HOTEL IS a world-class beach resort located on Kiawah Island. I have never been inside or even seen the front entrance, so I can't give any endorsement there. But I must say that the pool area is top notch. And while I didn't actually get a chance to take a dip, I highly recommend the lounge chairs.

Another wonderful feature of the Sanctuary that I enjoyed is their 24-hour EMT staff person. Although I can imagine it being quite a dull job the majority of the time, I think it's safe to say that the night of May 29, 2005 was an exception to the rule. I can just imagine the report that the couple by the pool gave when they found the EMT. "There's a big naked guy out there, and he needs your help."

It felt as if almost no time had passed before I saw her jogging out to me, with my two friends from the pool trailing close behind. Relieved to see help finally on its way, I found it easier to relax and tried to breathe as normally as possible. While each swallow of air still stung sharply in my chest, I managed to find a bit of a rhythm.

I knew as soon as the EMT arrived that the inquisition would begin, so I carefully considered what to say. I wanted to be truthful, but I also didn't want to dump a whole lot of information on this girl about LSD and Jesus and about how, up to about eight hours ago I had been the Messiah, but how I wasn't anymore. No, I needed to keep it as short and sweet as possible.

Sure enough, not a moment after the EMT reached my chaise lounge, the dreaded question came.

"What happened?"

While I hadn't settled on exactly how much information to give, I did at least know where to start.

"I, um, swam here."

Nice work, I thought. *That sounded about right.* Since more than anything, I really just wanted some water, she would now at least know that I was thirsty. It occurred to me, though, that my answer lacked one very important detail. I had not given any indication as to how long I had been swimming. For all she knew, I may have just been out for a quick dip. And since I certainly didn't want one of those puny little water bottles they give out at cocktail parties, I decided that I'd better qualify my statement.

"...from Folly Beach."

If she was tracking with me before, this is where I officially lost her. She looked at me sideways for a moment and then shifted her glance toward the ground. She seemed perplexed, as if she were trying to work out a difficult math problem in her head. I decided that she must have been processing whether or not my statement could possibly be true because she came to a quick conclusion, and her face grew stern.

"I'm here to help you," she began after a brief pause, "but you have to tell me the truth. What *really* happened?"

Since talking had proved to be quite difficult, I knew I wouldn't be able to provide her with any kind of satisfactory explanation. I thought about caving in and telling her what she wanted to hear—that I was a drunken skinny dipper—to see if she would be contented and bring me some water. But ultimately I needed more help than just a drink, so I racked my brain for a way to let her know that I meant business.

"Call my parents," I continued. "They'll explain."

Although her harsh look didn't lift, she did pull out a pad and a pen. She appeared ready to write, so I gave her my home telephone number. Whether she believed me or not, she would undoubtedly get the picture once she called the house. In fact, she probably had no idea that she was about to become the bearer of good news for my entire family. She uttered a quick word of reassurance and set off jogging back toward the hotel.

By this point, the couple from the pool had taken a seat across the deck and were monitoring the scene from a distance. They watched as the EMT disappeared out of sight and then turned their gaze back toward me. I caught their glance and lifted my hand to acknowledge their presence. They gave me a smile like one would a hurt puppy.

I closed my eyes to rest, and before I knew it, the EMT had returned. I opened my eyes to find her hovering over me with a bottle of water in one hand and a Gatorade in the other. Her face had softened up quite a bit, and she even flashed me a little smile. She had clearly called the house.

"I spoke with your parents," she said reassuringly. "They're on their way. I also called an ambulance."

She sat on the corner of the lounge chair as I chugged both the Gatorade and the water in a matter of seconds. She then waited with me for help to arrive. The ambulance showed up first, and two men came jogging out toward us. They must have been in cahoots with my EMT friend because they launched in with the exact same question that she had half an hour before.

"Sir, can you tell us what happened?"

Before I could even reply, the EMT interjected and gave them a brief synopsis.

"He swam here from Folly Beach and has been swimming all day," she began. "He is dehydrated and exhausted and may have aspirated some water as well."

They looked at her for a moment in silence, then immediately turned back to me. The man who had posed the question clearly did not like her answer and was not shy about letting us know. He told us that they did not drive all the way out to Kiawah to mess around and demanded that we tell the truth. I guess he just assumed that this resort EMT must be the most gullible person on the planet and that she had bought my story hook, line and sinker. He, on the other hand, would not be duped so easily.

"We're not going anywhere until you tell us what really happened," he continued.

Since I had no concept of what to do, I looked over at my EMT friend for help. She didn't seem to know how to respond either, so I started thinking of what I might say to win him over to our side. As I studied his unflinching face, I suddenly caught a glimpse of humor in the situation and felt a smile creeping up on me. I couldn't help it, so I just grinned and shrugged my shoulders.

Not real pleased with this response, the man sprang to his feet from where he had been crouching by my chair and pulled his colleague to the side. Fortunately, they were only huddled for a minute or so before my parents and older brother arrived.

As my family approached, they were clearly beside themselves. They had driven all this way on a phone call and a word from this EMT they had never met before. Now they wanted to see me for themselves. Finally, they caught sight of me lying on the chair, and a visible wave of relief washed over them. It was as if they had been holding in an entire day's worth of sighs and then let them go all at once.

Instantly, the tension lifted from the entire scene, and the tears began to flow. The nightmare was over. The mood on the deck changed as a wave of peace washed over the place, and even the couple from the pool, who were now locked tightly in an embrace, appeared to be moved by the display of emotion.

My mom took a seat beside me on the chaise lounge as the ambulance crew hurried off to get a stretcher. She could see how difficult it was for me to breathe and encouraged me not to speak. *Everything is going to be alright*, she said with her eyes. I laid my head back down and looked over at my father and brother who were hovering a few feet away. I gave them a quick nod and then closed my eyes to rest.

Before I knew it, I was staring at the roof of the ambulance on the way to hospital. They took me directly to Intensive Care, where I spent the rest of the night. And although I don't remember much about the next 24 hours, two things really stick out in my mind: oxygen and morphine. Just minutes after my arrival, they placed an oxygen tube under my nose and a morphine drip in my arm, and for the first time all night, I could literally breathe easy.

While I had been able to get some rest up to this point, both on the pool chair and in the ambulance, the pain in my chest had been so severe that I didn't want to let my guard down completely. Yet now that I was in good hands, I knew that I had no more reason to worry. I felt a great sense of release wash over my entire being, and I slipped off into a sleep that was deeper than any I have ever known.

∞   MIRACLE   ∞

WHEN I FINALLY AWOKE, I was alone. The white-washed hospital walls seemed to blend one into the next as if there were no corners at all, but rather one continuous barrier standing between me and the outside world. The clock on the wall read 3:30, but since all of the blinds were drawn, I had no concept of whether it was day or night.

I began to watch the second hand of the clock slowly and methodically tick away the precious moments of my new life. There was something extremely comforting about the regularity of its movement, and I eventually closed my eyes in order to just absorb the gentle sound. After a moment, my eyes shot open. I had forgotten to check one very important thing. I slowly leaned to one side of the bed and peered over the edge. *There it is!* I thought as I breathed a sigh of relief. *I'm back on solid ground!*

A wave of giddiness washed over my entire body, and I started to laugh. *I'm on the ground,* I repeated to myself. *I'm alive!* I wanted to pinch myself to make sure that I wasn't dreaming. For hours I swam with no hope of ever seeing this moment, and here it was. I only wish I could describe the pure joy I felt.

Instead, imagine for a moment that you have been paralyzed from the waist down from a car accident years ago. Every day of your life, you move directly from your bed into your wheel chair, which is your sole means of mobility. Your life is filled with unique challenges that are a direct result of your handicap, yet you have come to terms with the fact that this is how it will always be for you.

Now imagine one day you awake to find your legs miraculously healed. You eagerly test your new dexterity, moving your hips and bending your knees and wiggling your toes all at the same time. You discover all of it to be in good working order, so you leap out of bed and kick your wheelchair to the side. All day long, you can't stop dancing and running and jumping and twirling everywhere you go. Pure joy permeates your every step.

For weeks, nothing can get you down as you continually celebrate the simple gift of working legs. Every morning for years to come, as soon as you climb out of bed and stand on two feet, you remember what your life was like before. Gratitude floods your heart and remains there all day long, until your very last conscious moment before you fall asleep again.

This is the best way I can think to describe how I felt that day in my hospital room, and honestly how I still feel to this day. Each morning when I awake, I thank God for the ground underneath my feet and the breath that is in my lungs. These are two things I never thought I would have again—and two things I will never again take for granted.

Of course, some days are better than others, but being grateful is a choice I make every day. As a result, I have come to the realization that no matter what happens to me today, whether for good or for bad, nothing can outweigh the simple gift of being alive.

While my life was a miracle from the day of conception, I had never before acknowledged it as such. I always took for granted the fact that I possessed a sound mind and a functioning body. I never gave a second thought to the incredible gift of consciousness and my ability as a human being to interact with the world in a countless array of unique ways. I never appreciated life much because it was something that I had always had, and I simply could not imagine it ever being taken from me.

Thus, it wasn't until my second miracle that I began to understand how precious life truly is. I realized that as an amateur swimmer, the chances of surviving an episode like mine were slim to none. The simple fact that my body did not shut down from fatigue during 18 hours of swimming in the ocean is baffling all by itself, particularly in light of the fact that I hadn't slept a wink the night before. And that's not even counting any of the other factors—a jellyfish sting, a shark bite, even a simple muscle cramp—which could have ended my swim in an instant.

Where on earth did I get the strength? I continued to ask myself.

How am I still alive? Depending on your experience in the water, 18 hours may or may not sound like a long time to you. Either way, there is an easy way to find out for yourself. The next time you go for a swim at the neighborhood pool, make your way to the deep end and tread water for 30 minutes or so. You'll get the idea pretty quick.

Or consider my swim in light of the fact that it takes a trained swimmer 14 hours on average to cross the English Channel. As I mentioned earlier, I had been on the swim team at the local YMCA until I broke my arm when I was nine. I didn't swim another lap until I was 15, when I went through lifeguard training. In order to pass the course, we were required to complete a 500 meter swim, and my arms felt like Jello for days. That was the last time I swam any considerable distance before May of 2005.

Although 500 meters seemed like a long way at the time, it really does not stack up next to the Strait of Dover, which at 21 miles wide is the narrowest and most popular crossing point of the English Channel. Since I swam out and back rather than straight across, it is impossible to know exactly how far I traveled during my day at sea. But considering that I landed seven miles from where I started as the crow flies, I can safely say that it was my longest swim to date.

As I began to talk to the doctors and nurses in the hospital about my time in the ocean, I gained an even deeper appreciation for my miraculous survival. After 18 hours in the ocean, I was severely dehydrated, I had developed a stomach ulcer, there was salt water in my lungs, I was sunburned from the waist up, I had caught hypothermia and there was so much creatine kinase in my bloodstream, which is a protein from muscle breakdown, that the doctors were afraid my kidneys might fail.

Normal values of creatine kinase in the body are between 60 and 400 units per liter. For a runner who has just completed a marathon, levels would typically be somewhere in the low thousands. After my swim, the creatine kinase level in my body was 15,000 units per liter. The hospital staff said that it was by far the highest they had ever seen.

They decided to hold me in the hospital until my levels dropped below 10,000, which took four days. Even then, my arms were like lead weights, and my body still felt as if it had been run over by a Mack truck. The skin on my face was leathery like snake skin, and it continued to peel for another week more. Yet the biggest surprise of all came when I first stepped onto a scale. I went in the water at 225 pounds and now weighed a mere 205.

While this would be a great time to plug my new miracle weight-loss technique, I think it best to go in the opposite direction and provide a disclaimer—there are healthier ways to lose weight. May I suggest a diet that's rich in whole grains, fruits and vegetables? It will probably take longer than 18 hours to get the results you're looking for, but it will certainly leave you feeling better in the end.

All things considered, my survival in the ocean was nothing less than a modern-day miracle, and it is plain to see the supernatural hand of God at work. Even the course of my swim goes beyond mere coincidence. I swam unwittingly from Folly Beach to the Sanctuary Hotel—from folly to the sanctuary. A quick look at these two words shines light on the uncanny significance.

The Merriam-Webster Dictionary defines "folly" as: 1) a lack of good sense or normal prudence and foresight; 2) criminally or tragically foolish actions or conduct; 3) a foolish act or idea; or 4) an excessively costly or unprofitable undertaking. By contrast, "sanctuary" is defined simply as: 1) a consecrated place or 2) a place of refuge and protection.

Despite my years of folly, God never gave up on me and ultimately brought me back to his sanctuary. No matter how far away I tried to run, or rather swim, he was there all along. Like

Jonah, I had been swallowed up and spit back out—and given a second chance to get it right.

∞ A HOPELESS CASE ∞

THROUGHOUT MY TIME AT the hospital, a seemingly constant stream of family and friends blew in and out of my room like a revolving door. Some brought gifts, others an encouraging word and still more came just to sit by my side and keep me company. I told my story again and again, fielding every question under the sun from how long I had tripped to what the cops said to me on the beach to whether or not I got burned "down there"—the answer to which, I might add, is a big fat negative.

In addition to the often lengthy Q & A sessions, I also heard numerous accounts from friends and family about their experiences during my day at sea. Since I had been so singularly focused on my own survival during the swim and even while in the ICU, I had not given much thought to what the scene had been like back at home.

At first, I wasn't even sure when my family had learned of my disappearance. They were accustomed to me spending the night out without notice, and it wouldn't have been anything strange for me to miss church, even after promising I would be there. In fact, it could have easily been mid-afternoon before they began to suspect that something might be wrong.

Yet as it turns out, soon after I dove into the water, my jeans washed ashore with my wallet still in them. The police officers who had confronted me on the beach found it and contacted my parents. I have an extremely close-knit family, and word spread quickly. In addition to aunts and uncles and cousins coming over to the house to console my parents and older brother, I found my way onto nearly every prayer list in town within a matter of hours. And it being Sunday morning, I even got prayed for during several church services.

Charleston can be a very small town when it wants to be, and this was one of those times. My parents' house was filled with people coming and going all day, and the phone rang nonstop. Word spread like wildfire through the community, and everyone within about three degrees of separation heard of my disappearance at some point during the day. The local news even ran a five o'clock story on me.

Although there was not much to report, a local non-profit called the Coastal Crisis Chaplaincy acted as an informational relay between my family and the Coast Guard throughout the day. They provided real-time information about the status of the search and reassured my parents that everything within their power was being done to see me home safely.

But after hours of scanning the water with no success, both by boat and by helicopter, the Coast Guard was forced to call off their search midway through the afternoon. Not long after, a group of volunteer rescue workers began to comb Folly Beach in search of my dead body. One of these divers was a classmate I played soccer with in high school, who searched for hours before learning that it was my body he had been looking for all day. He later sent me the following account of his experience:

We searched two miles of ocean front and inlet, 150 yards off shore, thinking we would find a dead body eight feet below. I was circled by sharks twice and rescued another guard who was pulled from our chain in the inlet current. [...] But I did not find you. I knew with confidence that you were not in my waters. It was only a little help to know that you were not dead in the local water, but it was hope.

As the night wore on, though, that hope dwindled to practically nothing, and the reports that had been circulating all day became more and more definitive in nature. Friends started to receive phone calls informing them, not of my disappearance, but of my confirmed death. Our house slowly cleared of all visitors, and my parents finally decided to at least make an attempt to get some rest.

Yet while all hope seemed to be lost, the prayers continued to go up on my behalf. People I had never met, who knew nothing about me other than the fact that I was swimming for my life, who were scattered all over Charleston and God only knows where else, all fervently petitioned the Lord for my salvation. I believe with all of my heart that those prayers saved my life.

Although I had no awareness of it at the time, I found out later that the only reason why I had been able to make it back to land was because of a tide change that occurred just after 5 p.m., from outgoing to incoming. God heard the cries of his people, and I swam with the tide to safety.

About three years later, I met a pair of ladies from my aunt and uncle's church in Mt. Pleasant who had prayed for me that day. The first woman began by relaying her experience to me, sharing how upset she had been by my circumstance and how she had prayed all day long for my safe return.

After a brief pause, the second woman caught my eyes and asked quite casually, "How'd all that turn out for you?" I couldn't help but laugh. I thanked them profusely for their prayers and told them how the experience had turned my life around. They were overjoyed to hear the positive report and to see me, literally and figuratively, back on solid ground.

The night of my disappearance, my parents went to sleep with the almost certain assumption that I would be lost to them forever. The only phone call they were expecting to receive at this point was the one informing them of when and where my dead body had been found. Yet no more than 10 minutes after they had crawled into bed, the phone rang at the house.

My mother picked up to find a skeptical EMT on the other end who announced that she was calling from the Sanctuary Hotel on Kiawah Island. She apologized for phoning so late, but as she told my mom, there was a naked guy on the pool deck at the hotel who had given her this number and requested that she call. All of 45 seconds later, my parents were in the car with my brother racing at break-neck speed to Kiawah Island.

∞   To Keep You From the Bottom of the Sea   ∞

DUE TO THE BIZARRE NATURE of my story, I made some interesting local media appearances the following day. First, there was the newspaper article quoting a Coast Guard official who had explained how trying to find a person lost at sea was like trying to find a basketball in the middle of the ocean. Obviously there was some confusion between interview and article because the reporter went on to tell how I had used a basketball to keep me afloat all day.

A couple of local morning radio personalities also caught wind of my story, finding it amusing enough to discuss at length. According to a friend who caught the segment, these hosts could not get over the thought of a naked guy walking up the boardwalk of the Sanctuary Hotel at midnight to ask for a towel. How they acquired this bit of information, I do not know, but fortunately my name was not mentioned, and my friend didn't even realize that the story was about me until later in the day.

Yet aside from being fodder for the local news, I had managed to escape from my traumatic ordeal remarkably unscathed. I did not want to gloss over this fact. I had made a promise to God at a time when I literally had no ground to stand on, and he had come through in a big way. Now that my feet were back on solid footing, the real question was, would I keep my end of the bargain?

I've heard that part of loving God is to love the people around you, and I knew that my parents would be the place to start. I had inflicted them with the single most painful day of their lives, and although I knew that I would never be able to undo that damage, I resolved to do all in my power to make things right with them.

My parents had spent an entire day on pins and needles, waiting by the phone and wondering if they would ever see their youngest son again. I desperately wanted them to know how sorry I was for that day and to reassure them that I would never put them through something so terrible again. My experience in the water had changed me on the inside, and I longed for them to understand.

Ultimately, though, I realized that the true test of any internal change is its outworking into external action. If this conviction of my heart failed to alter my behavior for the better, then what would be the point? Now was the time to prove to my parents, and to everyone else, that I was indeed a new man.

While I knew for certain that God would be the source of my life-transformation, I still didn't really know where to start. I had a vague concept from my childhood about what God was like, and I had also learned a few things about his nature during my ordeal. Yet if I was going to see major change occur, I realized that I would need a much bigger piece of the puzzle than this.

I had spent a lot of time in the hospital daydreaming about what God was like, but in the end, it had not gotten me very far. I wanted something more tangible and concrete, something that I could sink my teeth into. As I considered where to begin, a thought popped into my mind that hadn't come up in years.

It had to do with a church retreat that I attended in high school called "Happening." Held at a local summer camp, this weekend getaway focused on helping kids develop a relationship with God. At the time, I didn't care a thing about God and went solely for the girls. Yet all these years later, I remembered that I had been given a Bible there, and barring the possibility that my parents had chucked it out during a bout of spring cleaning, it should still be in my closet.

As soon as I got home from the hospital, I headed for my room and swung open my closet door. Sure enough, I found the Bible right where I had left it five years prior. It sat on the second to top shelf, in a corner between a box of old toys and two shoeboxes full of old letters. As I reached up to grab it, a cloud of dust filled the air. With its pink and black cover, this was certainly not the manliest Bible I had ever come across. But at least I knew it would be a more modern translation than the King James Version we had in the living room.

As I pulled it down, I noticed something out of the corner of my eye and looked just in time to see a note about the size of an index card fluttering to the floor. I stooped down to pick it up and found a beautiful print of a sailboat at sunset on the one side and a short handwritten note on the other.

I read the note halfway through and stopped dead in my tracks. I could not believe my eyes. I read it over and over again before finally breaking my stupor. I peered around the room in disbelief, half expecting someone to jump out from behind the door to inform me that this was some kind of practical joke. The note read word for word:

Matt, the Bible is God's chart for you to steer by, *to keep you from the bottom of the sea*, and to show you where the harbor is, and how to reach it without running on rocks or bars.

Whoa. The note had been written by my first serious girlfriend and had been collecting dust in my closet for the past five years. The text was originally penned by Henry Ward Beecher, and when I finally got the chance to ask my former girlfriend about it years later, she had no recollection of the note or the quotation.

To keep you from the bottom of the sea! I chuckled to myself. *Unbelievable!* To me, the incident was quite hilarious, and I started laughing like I had that first day in the hospital. *God, you are too much!* I carried the Bible over to my bed, where I began reading from the book of Proverbs. And while I don't remember exactly what chapter or verse I read that day, I do remember the lesson I learned.

If God could plant a note like that five years in advance—then he could do anything.

∞   MATTHEW, GIFT OF GOD   ∞

IT WAS THE MORNING OF my first Sunday after being released from the hospital, and I knew that I had a choice to make. My experience with the note in my Bible had solidified my faith in God, and I found myself eager to learn more about this supernatural being who was able to orchestrate such an incredible coincidence. For the first time in my life, I actually wanted to go to church.

At the same time, though, I knew that if I were to show my face at my parents' church, the church I grew up in, I would get mobbed. I could just imagine the little old ladies crowding around, listening on with their hearing aids cranked up, genuinely trying to grasp the story. "L—S—what?" they would surely ask.

Not that they weren't well-meaning folks. In fact, the reason I knew they would make a fuss over me is because they cared about me. That being said, I wasn't quite ready to be a Sunday morning spectacle. I asked my parents for their opinion, and they suggested that we simply visit a different church.

As we deliberated about where to go, a family friend came to mind who had recently started working at a church on the way out to Kiawah, near where I swam ashore. Since we had yet to visit him there, we decided that this would be an ideal time. Not only would we be completely anonymous, we would get to support our friend as well as retrace the steps of my family's journey only a week before.

Although traditionally we weren't the most punctual churchgoers, we left the house early that morning to give ourselves plenty of time. The drive to the church took us through John's Island and some of the prettiest undeveloped land left in the Charleston area. Much of the way is still covered by massive live oak branches joining from either side to form a canopy over the road. *What a way to start the morning!* I felt an incredible sense of peace come over me long before we even arrived at the church.

We pulled into a gravel parking lot that was about half-full and began meandering our way to the church building. The property was beautiful, so we lingered for a few sweet moments, gazing at the massive old trees and drinking in the spring air. Before we had made much headway, we spotted our pastor friend whom we had come to visit. He had seen us as well and was already making his way out toward us.

As he drew near, I could see that his eyes were filled with tears. While he was not normally the gushy emotional type, I had learned from my time in the hospital that people react to these kinds of cataclysmic events in all sorts of interesting ways. In fact, it was moving to see such care and concern written so plainly on his face.

After greeting my family, he stood directly in front of me and placed his hands firmly on either side of my shoulders. His burning eyes met mine for just a moment, although it seemed like much longer, and then he drew me into an embrace. He spoke to me what a miracle it was that I stood before him and seemed to barely get the words out.

Once he released me from his grasp, he remained there with us for a few seconds, staring at me and slowly shaking his head. It was as if he truly could not believe his eyes. After a moment, though, he returned to his senses and informed us that he was needed to prepare for the service. He turned to leave, but stopped after only a couple of steps, looking back and shaking his head one final time in disbelief. "Just wait till you hear the sermon," he said with a great big smile on his face.

We decided it was about time to pick up our pace as well and proceeded to follow him into the church. Despite the traditional appearance of the building itself, the sanctuary had a modern feel to it, with red cushioned chairs in place of pews and a projector screen scrolling words to the pre-service music on the wall beside the altar.

After surveying the room, we noticed that there were plenty of seats and chose an empty aisle about halfway to the front, nodding as we sat to an older couple on the row in front of us who had turned around to say good morning.

Immediately after we were settled, I started to feel a genuine sense of excitement that I could not pinpoint. The encounter outside had made me curious about the sermon, and I found myself looking forward to the service rather than counting the minutes until it was time to leave. Let's just say I had never experienced a feeling of anticipation, at least the good kind, in church before.

Once the service started, my nerves settled a bit. After standing for a short prayer and a few worship songs, we sat while our friend took his place at the front of the church. He took a deep breath, glanced briefly in our direction and began his sermon entitled, "Matthew, Gift of God."

My eyes instantly filled up with tears. I looked over to my mom, and she was full-on bawling. Over the course of the next 20 minutes, I heard the phrase "Matthew, gift of God" repeated more times than I could count. Each time, it hit me like a wave of energy that resonated to the very core of my being. The words just washed over me, and I found myself completely lost in the moment. I knew beyond the shadow of a doubt that God was right there with us.

I learned later that the sermon was based on verses from the Bible that had been determined beforehand by something known as a lectionary. This is the schedule for the Sunday scripture readings that decides them in advance, not weeks or months, but years prior. As it turns out, my friend had absolutely no say in what passages to use for his sermon and even less of an idea that I would be attending the service.

For the second time that week, God came crashing into my life. The words did not boom like great peals of thunder, yet they did strike a chord deep inside of my soul. I found myself growing in awe of this supernatural being who was able to bring about such amazing events, deciding that "coincidence" was simply not a strong enough word. This was a "God-incidence."

Our worlds had collided, and I would never be the same for it.

CHAPTER SIX
_____

MORE THAN MEETS THE EYE

FOR THE THIRD TIME in one week, my world had been hit as if by a sledgehammer. First, I learned that God is not only real, but also extremely powerful. He appeared to be continually present and to actually know and care about me. And despite the fact that I had done everything in my strength to reject him, I was received back into his arms without so much as a harsh word.

Secondly, I learned that there is a reason why the Bible tops the best-seller list year after year. Far from being irrelevant and archaic, I discovered truth within those dusty pages that applied directly to my life as a college senior living in 21st century America. Before, I would have never in a million years expected that book to make it off my shelf. Now, it sat by my bedside.

Lastly, I had met with God in a most unlikely place, a venue that I had written off long ago—church. My previous impression of church was not far from that of grown men and women playing dress-up in order to carry forth a charade that dragged its victims through an endless cycle of fear and guilt. Now I was forced to revisit this distorted perception that had shaded my view of church since childhood.

I understood that if God is real and the Bible is relevant and church isn't a total sham, then I had better start reassessing my assumptions about life itself. Yet based on my previous experience with these things, I honestly did not expect much. As a child, I had concluded that God was scary, that church was boring and that the Bible did not make any sense. Plus, who wants to read a book that's chock-full of thees and thous?

In the end, though, I was ready to do just about anything to avoid revisiting the place of darkness I found beneath the ocean's surface. If the Bible had the power "to keep me from the bottom of the sea," then I was more than willing to give it a fair shot. I opted to stick with the modern translation from my closet and started reading a little each day, quickly realizing that my previous bias had been based almost entirely on secondhand information. In fact, I couldn't recall a single instance of trying to read the Bible for myself.

I have always taken a methodical and scientific approach to life, and I treated the Bible no differently. I scrutinized it page by page, and rather than discovering a mountain of contradictions as I had expected, I found an incredibly high level of consistency and truth. I saw that science, reason and academic study did not directly oppose the human quest for God as I once imagined they did. Instead, for the first time in my life, I found them supporting it.

I began to see concepts and principles from the Bible aligning with my observations of the natural world, and it seemed like the more I read and studied, the more I was able to understand the reality in which I found myself. The problem of human existence suddenly felt less like an obstacle and more like an opportunity. I discovered new answers to the age-old question of what the heck we're doing here floating around on a rock through space.

In addition to the Bible, I read other sacred texts in hopes of alleviating my negative sentiment toward religion as a whole. I looked for common threads running throughout the major world religions, from Christianity to Islam, Buddhism to Wicca. And although I found the differences largely to outweigh the similarities, I was able to identify one central element which appeared to be universal—the concept of faith.

So while the picture of God, or gods, portrayed by the various religions differs greatly, all seem to hold in common the idea that our human minds lack the capacity to fully comprehend the supernatural. This concept of the unfathomable nature of the spirit realm is prevalent in nearly every religious system I considered, but in no case did the problem of limited human understanding act as a hindrance to faith in its existence.

The more I thought about it, the more I realized that no human being understands everything they believe. We simply do not have the mental capacity. If complete understanding were a necessary component of belief, how could anyone say that they believe in gravitational theory or the theory of relativity? Not even the top scientists in the world are able to fully grasp the intricacies of these two theories, much less an Economics major like me. Yet we believe in them still.

That being said, we do not come to have faith in them blindly. Rather, we start with our set of empirical evidence and attempt to reconcile it with the theories in question. If we find overall alignment and are unable to identify any major inconsistencies, we may assent to belief. Thus, we allow reason to take us as far as it can and then step out in faith, trusting that Einstein and Newton actually knew what they were talking about.

Faith is a loaded word and one that six years ago would have caused me to withdraw from a discussion instantly. Nothing, I thought, could possibly be more unscientific than faith. But reality is we all operate on faith daily. How can we be sure that the front page of the newspaper or CNN.com is not complete baloney? The answer is that we can't. We choose to believe what we read only because we have faith in the validity of the source.

This same principle is true of the Christian Bible, the Tanakh, the Koran, the Bhagavad Gita, the Tao Te Ching, the Buddhavacana and every religious text ever written. In fact, it is true of all nonfiction, from science textbooks to ancient histories to my very own story. It is even true of the text message you got from your friend just a minute ago. Can you prove that she actually went to Target like she said? Of course not. Either you believe her, or you don't.

It turns out that nearly all of what we claim to know, the entirety of human knowledge itself, has been received at some point by faith. Everything outside of what we can see, hear, taste, touch or smell on our own is gained in this way. Otherwise, we would resign ourselves to know very little about the world in which we live. So perhaps having faith in God is not such a foreign concept after all.

Consider again the aforementioned religious texts. All of them have been recorded by real people in history who have chronicled specific encounters with the supernatural. Either we must write all of them off as human invention and complete fantasy, or we must acknowledge that the common thread running through them is simply too strong to ignore—and far too important.

In this vein, we must also take into account the sheer number of lives that have been transformed by the reading and studying of these documents throughout the ages. When I wrote God off as an invention of man designed to incite fear and keep people in line, I had no concept of the magnitude of my accusation. Yet now I see that it will take more than a conspiracy theory to adequately explain how billions of people living on this planet today profess to believe in some form of supernatural deity.

In the end, though, we are all given the same set of evidence and the same choice. Based on the information we have about the reality in which we find ourselves—including our observations of the natural world, the books we read, the people we talk to and even the thoughts inside our very own heads—we must all come to a conclusion about what we believe concerning the existence of God.

Let's be clear that this is not a choice between science and religion. The modern notion that the two can even be separated lacks historical perspective. Far from being mutually exclusive, these two disciplines have been interwoven throughout human history. From the Egyptian pyramids to the Mayan calendar to the rise of modern science in Europe, religion and scientific advancement have always fit hand in glove. Because what's the use of understanding the how without first knowing the why?

Take for example the age-old question of whether or not God created the universe. There are certain steps we can perform that will move us closer to making an informed decision. We can gather all of the evidence, read all of the books, carbon date all of the fossils and consider all of the theories—yet ultimately no one can travel back in time to watch how the world began. In this case, human reason and understanding are only able to carry us so far. We all inevitably reach the end of what we can know for sure, and at that point, we have no other option but to step out in faith and decide what it is that we believe.

Our choice is to believe either that life on planet earth is a product of randomness and chance or that it has been designed and created by a supernatural God. Either human consciousness is finite, produced solely by natural connections in the brain, or it is infinite, living on after the death of one's mortal body. Either "what you see is what you get" or "there is more than meets the eye." Either God is dead and nothing matters—or he is alive and human purpose remains.

No one can make this decision for us. We must all consider the evidence and choose a path for ourselves. And no one, regardless of how fervently they argue, can prove it one way or the other. Thus, even atheists must operate on faith to come to their conclusion that God did not make the world.

The question then is not *if* we choose to believe—but *what* we choose to believe.

∞ PARADIGM SHIFT ∞

AS MY FAITH IN GOD grew, I became increasingly aware of a roadblock that had for a long time stifled my openness to the spiritual realm. For as long as I could remember, I had believed wholeheartedly that human beings evolved from single-celled organisms and that all life on planet earth came into existence with zero outside input from God or anything else. This belief became the foundation for my atheism, leading me to conclude that life is finite and ultimately devoid of any real meaning or purpose.

During my entire educational career, from elementary school to college, I only remember evolution being presented in one way— as an undeniable fact of life. I never even knew there was a debate. The position that I heard over and over again in the classroom was precisely the position that I took as my own: How could anyone in their right mind believe anything else?

All that time, I remained completely unaware of the reality that there are actually two mainstream scientific theories of evolution, known as microevolution and macroevolution (notice only a one-letter difference). While the former is widely accepted, the latter continues to be a source of debate to this day among scientists, politicians, religious scholars and seemingly anyone scrounging for a good fight.

More often than not, when people use the term "evolution" unaided, they are referring to macroevolution. This simple oversight explains why so many debates on the subject quickly result in an impasse, because of a general neglect to properly define the terms. Only by separating these two distinct ideas will we be able to achieve any level of clarity on the matter.

The first theory, microevolution, represents an undisputed area of science that can be illustrated by Charles Darwin's famous observations during his visit to the Galápagos in 1835. During his time there, Darwin discovered several different populations of birds with unique characteristics living in groups scattered throughout the islands.

Deducing that they must have shared a common ancestor, Darwin developed a theory to explain how the birds became different. Over time, he concluded, these birds had adapted according to the food source available in their respective regions. In the places where food consisted of hard nuts that fell to the ground, the birds had developed short fat beaks, which they used to crack open the nuts. Where the primary food source consisted of grub burrowed deep inside of tree trunks, the birds had developed long thin beaks, which they used to extract the insects.

This phenomenon describes a simple change in gene frequency within a certain population. Birds born with the most advantage in their particular region—hard beaks in the one and long beaks in the other—were able to find the most food, thus giving them the highest likelihood of surviving and passing on their genes. Thus, these particular traits were "naturally selected" by the environment, allowing the birds to develop modified characteristics over time and evolve within their species.

While microevolution is an observable scientific principle supported by large bodies of evidence, of which the birds of the

Galápagos are merely one example, the second theory of evolution is much more speculative in nature. Known as macroevolution, or full-scale evolution, this theory contends that all living things, including human beings, arose over billions of years from single-celled organisms.

The reason why macroevolution is so problematic lies primarily in its reliance upon two difficult assumptions. The first assumption is that cellular life, the vitality which distinguishes organic beings from the non-organic, can somehow be created spontaneously. The second is that single-celled organisms can evolve into human beings when given a sufficient amount of time. Both of these assumptions carry with them an entire host of issues, preventing any kind of consensus from forming around macroevolution as a universally supported hypothesis.

Humans since the dawn of time have speculated whether life as we know it could possibly have created itself. Aristotle is cited as the originator of this notion that life can spring from inanimate matter, a theory later dubbed as spontaneous generation. This theory prevailed in science for more than two millennia and was used to explain how worms appeared in mud puddles after a rain storm and how maggots formed in rotting meat.

Although the theory was questioned and tested by skeptics as early as the 15th century, it was not fully debunked until 1859. That year, Louis Pasteur conducted his famous swan-necked bottle experiment, demonstrating that fermentation is caused by the growth of micro-organisms, not spontaneous generation. Pasteur believed that this antiquated theory had been laid to rest for good and in 1864 publicly announced, "Never will the doctrine of spontaneous generation recover from the mortal blow struck by this simple experiment."

For the first time in two thousand years, there was suddenly no alternative answer to the formation of life, barring intervention from a supernatural God. Science had performed its originally appointed duty, increasing human understanding of the world in which we live and thereby pointing society back to the undeniable existence of an intelligent creator.

Yet because the reality of God carries with it implications that extend beyond laboratory walls, a portion of the worldwide scientific community will always fight tooth and nail for a Godless explanation of life on this earth. For if God is not real, then nothing matters. And if nothing matters—then I can do whatever I want.

So as one guilty of intentionally suppressing the truth about God myself, it does not surprise me that merely a decade after Pasteur's "mortal blow" to spontaneous generation, the door to Godless creation theories would once again be thrown wide open. It does surprise me, though, how it was reopened—not in a laboratory, but with the simple stroke of a pen.

In a letter written to a friend in 1871, Charles Darwin suggested that the original spark of life may have begun in a "warm little pond, with all sorts of ammonia and phosphoric salts, lights, heat, electricity, etc. present, so that a protein compound was chemically formed." He went on to explain that "at the present day such matter would be instantly devoured or absorbed, which would not have been the case before living creatures were formed."

Thus in one fell swoop, Pasteur's nail in the coffin of spontaneous generation was successfully removed. Yet rather than retaining its original name, this debunked theory took on a new identity which remains to this day. Called "abiogenesis," it is simply the modern hypothesis that life on planet earth arose spontaneously from inorganic matter.

We learned from Pasteur's conclusive experiment that life cannot randomly manufacture itself on the earth under our present conditions. Thus, abiogenesis hinges on the conjecture that earth's early environment may have differed significantly enough from the one we inhabit today to allow for life to spontaneously appear.

Due to the relatively basic understanding of cellular life that existed around the turn of the century, this theory of abiogenesis would have seemed quite conceivable at the time of its proposal. To the scientific community of the day, a single cell was believed to be nothing more than a primitive blob of protoplasm that could have easily coalesced from foundational elements.

Yet advancements in the field of molecular biology, particularly in the last fifty years, have cast a long shadow of doubt on the plausibility of abiogenesis. A modern biochemical examination of the inner workings of living cells reveals a myriad of incredibly complex mechanisms, each resembling finely engineered machines that far outpace any human technology in terms of performance and efficiency. There are simply no conceivable working theories to properly explain how these intricate systems could have organized and created themselves.

In addition to the barrier of sheer complexity, there is also an inevitable chicken and egg problem that arises when tackling the spontaneous origin of cellular life. For example, one prominent origin-of-life theory asserts that RNA was spontaneously formed and then used to create the first living cell. But we know that outside of a cell membrane, RNA quickly decays—and that without RNA, it is impossible for a cell membrane to form. Therefore, it would be entirely unfeasible for one to develop independent of the other.

In fact, the absence of a plausible abiogenesis theory has driven some scientists over the years to look elsewhere for answers. In the early 1970s, Nobel prize winner Francis Crick became so skeptical of the likelihood that life on earth had spawned randomly that he suggested an alternative—perhaps the seeds of life had been sent to earth by an advanced extraterrestrial civilization, a theory known as panspermia.

Yet if abiogenesis shifts the spontaneous generation problem to "back then," alien theory only moves it to "out there." Plus, the fact that a prominent scientist such as Crick would acknowledge that a long-shot like panspermia holds more plausibility in his estimation than any of the other existing origin-of-life theories is extremely telling.

It appears that life on earth is too orderly, too complex and simply too well-designed to have spawned itself. As a friend once put it, "How can nothing create something?" Perhaps it is time to lay the theory of abiogenesis to rest—in the very same coffin Pasteur built for its predecessor, spontaneous generation.

Since the second assumption of macroevolution has no bearing without the first, I will not discuss it at length. But it is worth noting that one of the strongest bodies of evidence against macroevolution continues to be the lack of transitional fossils needed to show that life on earth has the capacity to evolve across species lines.

When Darwin proposed the theory of macroevolution toward the end of the 19th century, he recognized that the fossil record of his day lacked sufficient evidence to support his theory. He believed that over time, a multitude of transitional fossils would be unearthed, thereby validating his hypothesis that full-scale evolution did in fact produce human life. Yet more than a century later, modern archaeology has failed to produce a single transitional species, leaving us to grapple with glaring holes in the fossil record—and thus in the theory of macroevolution.

While I am not one for controversy, I would like to add my two cents to the Darwinism vs. Creationism debate. I speculate that if Charles Darwin were alive today, he would not believe his own theory. As a true man of science, I think he would take one look at the microbiological evidence and one look at the archeological evidence and conclude that it simply does not add up.

Don't get me wrong, I'm not trying to end the debate. Science will never be able to prove or disprove the existence of God, and everyone must choose what they believe for themselves. As for me, though, I have seen enough—and I am ready to move on.

∞ ALL ROADS ∞

IF THE WORLD WAS NOT created spontaneously, how then did it come into being? To answer this question, we have only to observe the incredible complexity that exists all around us. The universe and our planet are so intricately designed that it would be difficult to chalk them up to a random set of parameters aligning purely by accident. The evidence strongly suggests the existence of a supernatural creator.

We can easily see this principle at work in the natural world. Take a simple mechanical instrument like a watch for example. Any person in their right mind could look at such an object and determine that it had been designed and created by an intelligent person. Even if you were to dismantle the finished product into its corresponding parts, a skilled craftsman would be required to reassemble the watch if it were to ever work properly again.

In the same way, it is plain to see the craftsmanship and design that exist throughout our world. To think that the unfathomable expanse of the universe could be constructed of molecules and particles too small for the human brain to even conceptualize, all combining seamlessly to create life as we know it, is simply astounding. God's signature has been written into the very DNA of creation.

The question then that follows is, which God? Don't all religions essentially say the same thing anyway? Don't all roads lead to the same destination in the end? With so many different religious systems out there, how could we possibly sort through them all?

Let's start with the notion that all religions are essentially the same. The simple answer is that if all religions were the same, then they wouldn't be different religions. They wouldn't have different sacred texts and different practices and different moral standards. They wouldn't contradict one another, and we could simply go on believing whatever we want to believe.

Just like with the laws of physics, there are laws at work in the spiritual realm. Gravity holds us to the earth whether we believe in it or not, indeed whether we understand it or not. The physical laws of nature do not change simply based on what we think or believe about them. They are what they are and apply universally at all times.

The laws of the spirit work in much the same way. Either there is a God or there is not. Either there is a set moral standard or there is not. It cannot be both. So regardless of what you and I believe about these things, or what any individual or people group believes about them, the reality goes unchanged. Our perception of reality does not alter it.

The truth is that every major world religion self-separates from all of the others. Hinduism upholds the caste system as the way to Nirvana. Buddhism asserts that Nirvana is achieved through the eightfold path. In Taoism, The Way is the creator of all things. Zoroastrians believe the creator to be Ahura Mazda. Sacred writing in Judaism centers on the Old Testament, Christianity on the New Testament and Islam on the Koran.

Thus, if any one of the aforementioned religious systems is true, then the others cannot be. The belief that all religions are equally valid is a contradiction in and of itself. There are certainly common themes like the Golden Rule—do unto others as you would have them do unto you—but even that is not a universal standard. Let's just say that Satanists don't adhere to it.

Now let's not confuse the issue. All people deserve the freedom to pursue God however they choose. And all people are equally valuable in God's eyes. But it does not follow that all ideas are equally valid. So if Christians are right, then Buddhists are wrong. And if Muslims are right, Zoroastrians are wrong. And if I believe that pink elephants from outer space are going to swoop in and take me off to Candy Land, then I am in for a rude awakening.

Since all religions cannot be simultaneously true, how then are we to know which one, if any, is right? Living in the age of information, we have access to a mind-numbing amount of data about every topic imaginable, including world religion. We can read about anything from original doctrine and religious ceremony to modern day belief and practice, all with a simple Google search.

Yet there is one central measure for every world religion that has the potential to shed light on the whole tangled mess, and that is the subject of eternity. All of us have a finite lifespan, and death is not choosy. The only way for our lives to hold any significance is through the connection to an eternal reality.

Many religious systems center on finding happiness in the here and now. But unhappiness is not our greatest enemy—death is. Our mortality is the very reason why we need God. Many believe that the primary purpose of religion is to make people act better. And while behavior modification may be a result of religious practice, the main function of religion is to connect mortal man to eternal God.

Of the handful of eternity-centric religions, the vast majority uphold that the way to earn favor with God is through our actions here on earth. They go on to assert that at the end of our lives, we will be judged for what we have done. If our good deeds outweigh the bad, then we will be accepted by God and granted eternal life. But if the bad outweighs the good, we will be condemned and face eternal punishment.

Although this type of judgment seems reasonable at first glance, I do not believe that it is ultimately a just system. The dilemma with any spectrum-based assessment lies in the cutoff. At some point, a line must be drawn indicating who will be justified and who will be condemned. This means that one person could receive eternal reward for achieving a 70 percent score on the good deed meter and another face eternal punishment for only reaching 69 percent.

While this system may be adequate in grade school, it is no way to determine one's eternal fate. Two people with almost identical track records being separated for all of time does not sound like justice to me. Plus, how could someone in this model ever rest knowing that they may be one good deed short of eternal reward? How would they ever know when their righteous requirement had been satisfied?

There are many such world religions that proclaim a merit-based road to God and to eternal life. Yet there is one belief system that takes us in a completely different direction—Christianity. In the Christian faith, it is believed that there is no way to earn acceptance with God by our own merit. Since God is perfect, we would have to achieve perfection in order to meet his standard. We wouldn't need a 69 or 70 percent score on the test—we would need a 100.

Since it is impossible for us to do this on our own, Christians believe that God sent Jesus Christ to the earth to do it for us. The story goes that Jesus was the only human being in history to live a faultless life and to score a perfect 100, thereby earning entrance into God's eternal paradise. He then offered to share his perfection with all who aren't perfect but who follow him, a concept known as grace. Instead of us reaching up to God, God reached down to us.

Many people respect Jesus as a great ethical teacher, yet that is simply not what he taught about himself. Jesus claimed to be the son of God and the only way to gain eternal life. Either this is true, or he was a liar and a lunatic. A man who made the claims that Jesus did cannot be written off as just another moral leader. He simply does not give us that option.

And although this dilemma would be difficult to settle based on Jesus' words alone, we have something much more convincing to decide upon. Jesus is set apart not merely by his teachings, but by his resurrection from the dead. Some people follow Moses, some Muhammad, some Confucius, some Buddha, some Aristotle, some Socrates, some Joseph Smith and some Darwin. But what do they all have in common? They're all dead.

Yet Jesus is alive—and more than deserving of a closer look.

∞   EXIT STRATEGY   ∞

IN ORDER TO UNDERSTAND the Christianity story, we must begin at the beginning—the creation of the world. Recorded in the first chapter of the book of Genesis, the account chronicles how God formed the entire universe in seven stages, each described by the Hebrew word Yom. Literally translated "day," Yom can also be used to refer to a longer period of time or an era.

Although the description in Genesis chapter one is brief, the evidence of incredible order and complexity shines throughout. From the explosive big bang to the appearance of humans, the progression is utterly fascinating. And while I had been told my whole life that the account was obsolete, one reading of it proved enough to change my mind.

The story goes on in chapter two to illustrate how God formed the human race from the dust of the earth. It explains that the reason why he created us was to be in relationship with him and to live with him in the idyllic Garden of Eden. In that place, there was abundant food, rivers of clean water and no trace of suffering. Even the beasts lived at peace in God's presence.

There was work there but no toil, and the earth produced abundantly without thorns or weeds. There was no pain, no sorrow and no sadness of any kind. The first man and woman even walked around naked because they had no concept of shame or fear. In order to protect his children, God gave them one simple boundary with one simple consequence for disobedience. Don't eat of one certain tree. If you eat of it, you will die.

The story goes that a fallen angel tempted the first woman by questioning the command from God, and she and her husband both ate. The result of this first act of disobedience was more disastrous than they could ever have imagined. They immediately became aware of their nakedness and covered themselves with leaves that they found. They felt fear for the very first time and hid from God.

Since God is unchanging and perfect, he was unable to go back on the promise that he made. His children broke a direct command, and the consequence for their action was death. The man and the woman were dispelled from the Garden and sent out into the world we currently inhabit. They were separated from God and from his source of eternal life.

Although they didn't die at that very moment, Adam and Eve did ultimately perish. So have all of their offspring since. Through their decision to willfully disobey God, sin entered the world. Sin alters our entire state of being and distorts our view of reality and of God himself. It is what separates us from God, lying at the root of all fear, doubt, anxiety, guilt and shame. It is sin that leads to death.

The reason why sin is so devastating has to do with the nature of

God himself. The Bible says that God is holy, which means that he is perfect and set apart. God lives in a place that is eternally faultless. He wants us to live with him there, yet there is one problem. Since God is perfect, he is unable to dwell in the presence of sin.

Thus, in our present state, not a single human being on the planet would be able to enter heaven. Just as sin has infected our entire world, if one imperfect human were allowed into the next world, the sanctity and holiness of that place would be compromised forever. Heaven would cease to be heaven, and the entire point of salvation would be lost.

But since God so desperately wants us to spend eternity with him, he has created a way for us to enter his realm without compromising his holiness. Rather than lowering his perfect standard to graft us in, God sent his son Jesus Christ into the world to meet the righteous requirement of heaven. By living a perfect and sinless life, Jesus earned the right to live with God forever.

Unfortunately, this is only half of the equation. The penalty for our sin still had to be paid, which is why Jesus had to die on the cross. Despite his complete innocence, he took on the punishment for our crimes. And although it would be impossible to fully know the price that Jesus paid on the cross for us, we can begin to explore the depth of his sacrifice by recounting the physical agony that he suffered.

Jesus faced the worst treatment that human beings had to offer. He was whipped and scourged until no skin remained on his back. He was punched, kicked, spat upon, mocked and taunted. A crown of thorns pierced his skull. Three nails were driven through his body, two in his wrists and one through both of his feet. He suffocated while hanging atop a wooden cross. His dead body was then stabbed with a spear.

As gruesome as this description is, it doesn't even begin to scratch the surface of the ordeal Jesus endured. In that moment, he bore the weight of God's judgment against the sins of the entire world. He shielded the human race from the fate that we deserve and absorbed the most horrific punishment of all—he became separated from God.

The God who is the very author of life took on death. For three days, Jesus descended into the land of the dead until that first Easter morning when he rose back to life. The grave could not hold him because the life within him was too great. Through his resurrection, Jesus proclaimed his victory over death. And he offers to share that victory with all who follow him.

By his sacrificial death on the cross, Jesus broke the curse that began in the Garden of Eden and removed the barrier that stood between us and God. This is the good news that he came to share, that our sins have been forgiven. He has offered to clothe us in his righteousness so that we might meet the requirement for entry into heaven. He has made a way for us to live with God forever.

While Jesus offers salvation to all, it does come with a condition. In order to receive forgiveness for our sins, we must first repent of those sins. To repent literally means to turn around. It is a call to give up our selfish desires and surrender control of our lives to him. It means to abandon our hopes and our dreams in order to submit to the plan that God has for us.

Jesus is not an add-on, but a whole new direction. In order to receive the new life that Jesus has to offer, we must first die to the old. We must lay aside our own self-interest and embrace the all-encompassing love that Jesus demonstrated during his time on the earth. Repentance is a call to reorder our entire lives, to restore God to his proper place in our hearts and to put the needs of others before our own.

The moment we repent and give our mortal lives to God, he

meets us with eternal life. This new life does not begin when we die physically, but rather when we die in spirit to our old way of life. In that instant, we are able to be born again of God's spirit and receive his unending life. We can do this at any time through repentance— but once the exchange has been made, there is no turning back.

God has given every one of us a window of time to repent of our sins and receive forgiveness, namely our mortal lifespan. Not a single one of us knows when our time will be up or if we will even live to see tomorrow. This is why it is so important to take action today. The journey is not an easy one, but it is the only way to true and lasting fulfillment. Jesus Christ is the only person on the planet who can walk with us through life and right on through death.

As long as we still have breath in our lungs, we can make the trade. I cried out to God with my dying breath in the water, and he saved me. I had been stripped of everything—alone, naked and exhausted—sinking into an eternity of doom. All I had left was a single breath to cry out to God. And the amazing thing is that he made the exchange even then.

Now there are others who cry out on their death beds and who do not survive. They receive eternal life without their mortal lives being spared. I was given both, and I know the reason. I am alive to share what I saw in the water, that death is not an end but a beginning. I am alive to share the good news of Jesus Christ.

You may be saying that there is no harm in waiting. Yet no one knows when that day will come. You could get in a car accident this afternoon and die instantly. Hopefully you won't, but the point is that you never know. What you have right now will not last. Whether your lot in life is good or bad, you cannot keep it. The grave spares no one.

The Bible says that on the day of final judgment, we will all stand before the throne of God. The entire earth and the sun and the moon and the stars will be wiped away. All of our material possessions and our accolades and our fancy job titles will crumble like dust. We will be seen for what we truly are on the inside, and the state of our hearts will be revealed.

Those who have repented of their sins will be clothed in the righteousness of Christ and allowed to enter the eternal kingdom of God. They will live with him forever in perfect peace and joy and love. Those who have not repented of their sins, on the other hand, will not be able to meet the righteous requirement of God and will be unable to enter God's paradise.

It has become an unpopular position in our culture to assert that there is only one way to God. But unless we repent, our sins cannot be forgiven. And unless our sins are forgiven, it is impossible for us to enter God's eternal kingdom. In order to protect his perfect home, God must refuse entry to all who do not receive forgiveness and salvation through Jesus Christ. Although God still loves them, they will be forced to spend eternity separated from him in hell.

The good news is that God doesn't want any of his children to go to hell. He desires for every single one of us to spend eternity with him in heaven. This is why he sent Jesus to save us. Jesus entered into our world to give the offer of salvation to all who would repent and believe—and then he rose from the dead to prove that his words were true. He is coming back to the earth at the end of time to bring justice to the nations and to judge the living and the dead. He has always been and will always be the way to God and heaven, and his offer of eternal life is on the table.

The only question left is, will you take it?

EPILOGUE

It has been more than six years since I made my promise to God in the ocean, and I remain completely sober from drugs and alcohol. It was a pledge that under any other circumstance would have been impossible for me to keep, yet God delivered me from all desire to return to my old life, including premarital sex, internet pornography, gambling, lying, cheating and stealing. I have seen where that road ends, and I am determined never to return. What's more, I have experienced the love of God in Jesus and know that there is truly nothing better.

My swim in the ocean was a baptism of sorts, and through it, I experienced a rebirth of water and of Spirit. On the shore of Kiawah Island, I came alive in a way that I never before thought possible. I was overwhelmed by a sense of pure joy simply from being back on solid ground. God began to change me from the inside out, giving me eyes to see all of the blessings he had bestowed upon me over the course of my life. I realized for the first time how each new day on this earth is a gift and found a fully renewed sense of appreciation for my family, my friends, my home and even my tired, sunburned body.

As I walked with Jesus day by day, he gave me an awareness of the damage I had done to others, both through my swim and during the out of control spiral leading up to it. I desperately wanted to rebuild my broken relationships and felt him calling me to start at home. I began looking for ways to bless my parents through random acts of kindness and discovered that I had a new capacity to love in a way I never before thought possible. And the most amazing thing about this change of heart toward my parents was that it did not feel like a chore. Grateful for the decades of love and self-sacrifice they had poured out into my life, I enjoyed blessing them. If anything, I only wished I could do more.

In addition to my parents, I reached out to other family and friends to apologize for what I had put them through. Over the following weeks and months, I saw genuine reconciliation happen right before my eyes. One by one, my relationships were restored. I learned the importance of forgiveness and sought to release those who had hurt me in the past from the resentment and bitterness I had held toward them. I realized how much hostility I had been carrying, literally since the sixth grade, and felt all of that weight being lifted from my shoulders. This sense of release has continued to increase over time, to the point where I can honestly say that I harbor no ill will toward any of my high school or college classmates—or anyone else for that matter—and that I wish them all the very best.

At the end of my quiet summer at home, I returned to college for my senior year. Since I had already signed a lease to live with my two best friends, I was daily confronted with my old lifestyle. Yet rather than being tempted and enticed by what I saw, I was repulsed by it. I felt ashamed of the incredible opportunity I had wasted over the prior three years, all for the sake of having a good time.

I spent a lot of time alone that year, reading and reflecting in the quiet of my room. As I learned about the character of Jesus through the Bible and through the Holy Spirit in prayer, I was drawn to him and desired to be more like him. Meditating on the image of Jesus helped to renew my mind, and the more his goodness grew on the inside, the more it manifested itself outwardly.

As the school year progressed, I found new sources of community through a campus ministry as well as a local church, both of which helped to strengthen my faith greatly. The church I joined quickly became a transformative force in my life, but not just because of what happened inside the building. There was a group of homeless men who lived in the church parking lot, a place we all called "the hill," and over time, I befriended many of them. This happened mostly because they were impossible to miss, and because I always made a point of speaking to them as I went to and from the church.

Over the next few months, my two-minute conversations turned into five and ten minutes, until I found myself hanging out there for hours at a time. At first, they called me "preacher man" because I always carried my Bible and told them my story about how God had changed my life—and how he could change theirs too. Yet in due course, I found myself talking at them less and spent more time simply listening.

It took two full years, but God used those men to soften my heart. I began to see that they are no less valuable in his sight than I am, and the relationships I built in that church parking lot helped me to gain an entirely new perspective on the world. We certainly had our fair share of challenges, as life on the street is often fraught with difficulty, but I simply tried to love them the way Jesus would have.

Upon my graduation from college in 2006, I took a job with a local community economic development nonprofit. Through my work, I continued to learn about the plight of the poor and needy, and my compassion for others continued to grow. After two years of wrestling with the idea, I opened up my apartment to the guys from the hill. I would often have three of them sleep over at a time, one in my extra bedroom and two on my couches.

I saw incredible life change during that time and thought that I had found my calling. Then tragedy struck my family, and my dad was diagnosed with terminal cancer. I quit my job immediately and moved home to Charleston to help my mom care for him. Although our time together was short, less than four months in total, my relationship with my father grew like never before.

After his death, I remained at home to help my mother manage a small family business. For over two years, we ate together, worked together and supported each other daily. God used that time to redeem our relationship and to restore us to unity and peace. I can safely say that I have never been closer to anyone in my whole life, and I counted her as my best friend in the world.

Until, that is, I met Nicole. God brought us together in April of 2010, and we were married in June of 2011, nearly three years to the day after my move home to Charleston. During our time together, we have come to understand that love is not first a feeling, but an action. Just as Jesus laid down His life for us, Nicole and I seek to do for one another.

God's love is more amazing and powerful than any human could ever know on this side of death. In my six years of walking with the Lord, I have witnessed hope restored, peace beyond understanding, joy in unimaginable abundance, kindness overflowing, patience steadying, goodness overcoming evil, self-control protecting, gentleness tempering and faith leading the way.

The good news is that God has not given up on us. If we are willing to turn to him, he will receive us back into his loving arms, no matter how far we have strayed. He offers salvation to each and every one of us, every single day, without exception. There is no situation too hard for him and no darkness that his light cannot penetrate.

And hey, if God can save me—he can save anyone.

CPSIA information can be obtained at www.ICGtesting.com
Printed in the USA
LVOW040940181111

255539LV00003B/1/P